Paul Sams is a practicing property Solicitor actively involved in residential, residential and commercial development with niche specialisms in leasehold enfranchisement matters plus equity release.

A Practical Guide to Equity Release for Advisors

A Practical Guide to Equity Release for Advisors

Paul David Sams
LLB Hons (silver badge in Cycling proficiency)
Solicitor
Specialist in all matters Conveyancing both
Residential and Commercial

Law Brief Publishing

© Paul Sams

All rights reserved. No part of this publication may be reproduced, stored in a retrieval system, or transmitted, in any form or by any means, electronic, mechanical, photocopying, recording or otherwise, without the prior permission of the publisher.

Excerpts from judgments and statutes are Crown copyright. Any Crown Copyright material is reproduced with the permission of the Controller of OPSI and the Queen's Printer for Scotland. Some quotations may be licensed under the terms of the Open Government Licence (http://www.nationalarchives.gov.uk/doc/open-government-licence/version/3)..

Cover image © iStockphoto.com/gopixa

The information in this book was believed to be correct at the time of writing. All content is for information purposes only and is not intended as legal advice. No liability is accepted by either the publisher or author for any errors or omissions (whether negligent or not) that it may contain. Professional advice should always be obtained before applying any information to particular circumstances.

Published 2018 by Law Brief Publishing, an imprint of Law Brief Publishing Ltd
30 The Parks
Minehead
Somerset
TA24 8BT

www.lawbriefpublishing.com

Paperback: 978-1-911035-99-2

To Ethan and Noah, my sometime adorable children, who keep me grounded, keep me busy and teach me something new every day. Also to my supportive team at work who put up with me on a daily basis.

PREFACE

Thank you for reading this book. For those of you who think it is an introduction to "Equity" the Trade Union for actors then I am afraid you have come to the wrong place.

If however you are looking for guidance in how to deal with and act upon instructions regarding an equity release mortgage (from herein to be known throughout this book as an ERM to save my aching fingers having to type too much), then the contents of this tome will be of use to you. At least I hope they will.

The law stated in this book is believed to be correct based on information available to me up to 25th August 2018.

Paul Sams
August 2018

CONTENTS

Chapter One	Introduction	1
Chapter Two	What Is Equity Release?	3
Chapter Three	Advising Your ERM Clients	11
Chapter Four	Mental Capacity	31
Chapter Five	Undue Influence	51
Chapter Six	What if Someone Does Not Make Provision in Their Estate?	69
Chapter Seven	Joint Ownership	73
Chapter Eight	Conclusion	89
Appendix	Equity Release Council Resources	91

CHAPTER ONE
INTRODUCTION

Within the chapters of the book we will be taking a look at what an ERM is, the different types and the supposed perception of them by the legal profession as well as society as a whole. In addition we will take a look at some of the risks that can come into play regarding ERM's including mental capacity (specifically that of your clients' rather than your own), undue influence and joint ownership.

An awful lot of firm's don't undertake ERM work. Some may take it on and not realise that they are. One thing is for certain though – if you are a solicitors' or licenced conveyancers' practice that acts on such matters then your professional indemnity insurers will want to know.

If you are a Partner or supervisor within a firm then you will want to be able to ensure that your staff know the risks that an ERM presents. If they know the risk then they can take reasonable steps to mitigate the same. I have presented seminars on this topic across England on the same and it never ceases to amaze me some of the naivety shown by my profession towards ERM matters.

With an appreciation of the risks and simple procedures in place then you can make sure that as well as acting in the best interests of your clients then you are also protecting your respective firms. You will also be aware of the financial benefits to your firms in that if few people are experts in this field then "market forces" will allow you to charge for your time accordingly.

Financial advisors and others who also work in the ERM field may also find the following chapters of use as well. At least I hope they do.

Well without further ado, let's start by looking at what an ERM actually is.

CHAPTER TWO
WHAT IS EQUITY RELEASE?

Equity release is a means of retaining use of a house or other object which has capital value, while also obtaining a lump sum or a steady stream of income, using the value of the house. The "catch" is that the income-provider must be repaid at a later stage, usually when the homeowner dies. - https://en.wikipedia.org/wiki/Equity_release

So, we have a definition above which I think is pretty easy to understand. In a way this type of transaction has been taking place for years. Shakespeare had the use of someone offering something as collateral for a monetary loan as a plot device in the Merchant of Venice. Pawn broking has existed for centuries and modern banks and financial institutions are carrying on the same, albeit not asking for a pound of flesh, although some borrowers may feel that they may as well be.

Like all financial loans there are numerous options and variables involved with the availability as well as the intricacy relating to the same. There are certain key factors in all equity release schemes and these are:

- It is an interest only mortgage
- It has to be secured against your main residence
- You have to be over 55 years of age to obtain the same

As I have hinted at above there are various ways that the three fundamentals above can change. It is possible to find ERM products that allow capital repayment and some providers are considering allowing borrowers to secure an ERM against a second home. The one true fundamental I suppose is that you have to be over 55 years of age to qualify. The caveat on that for the future in my mind is that as the population gets older then that minimum age may need to be raised as life expectancy increases. I have myself acted for clients who have taken out, repaid and then taken out a further ERM.

So why do people take out an equity release mortgage? This is by no means a comprehensive list but in my experience the following covers why most clients look at ERM schemes:

- An easy way to obtain instant funds – provided the property is valued over £70,000.00 at the time of writing and subject to some basic mortgage underwriting criteria it is unlikely that an ERM product cannot be found for someone who wants one.

- To take money now to reduce the value of their estate for IHT purposes – personally I think this is perhaps a rare reason to take an ERM but people do.

- To help children out now rather than when they pass away – a client said to me once that he wanted his children to remember him for what he was when he was alive rather than what he left him when he had passed away. He (amongst) other clients I have acted for want to gift monies to their children (and others) whilst they are alive to see the benefit/enjoyment that others may have from it.

- To fund their lifestyle – living on the south coast as I do, then going on a cruise is expensive. As technology expands and the world gets smaller then those who have retired often want to keep to the lifestyle they had when they were working so ERM options allow them to live the life they want.

- Poor pension choices – hardly a day goes by without some scandal or another being revealed about pensions. Taking an ERM can alleviate issues surrounding the same.

- They need to repay another mortgage or other debts – it never ceases to amaze me the number of people I have spoken to over the years that assume that debts will just "disappear" when they retire or die. If a loan is still in place against a property or other assets that someone over 55 years of age may have the only option of taking an ERM.

- They have no choice – sometimes people have no way to be able to afford the cost of living without borrowing against their own home which is, more than often, the only significant asset they have.

So we have considered various options as to why ERM are an option for people. However, there are alternatives. It is important (we will look at this in more depth in the next chapter) to speak to your clients and make them aware that there are alternatives they may wish to consider. So what alternatives are there to equity release? Again not an exhaustive list but:

- They could sell their current home and buy somewhere else

- They could raise finance in another way

- They could see if their children or another third-party can help them financially

On the face of it I think we can agree that ERMs sound like a straightforward and effective solution to providing funds to the over 55s into their later lives. However, if you speak to many within the legal profession they will recoil in horror at the thought of acting for someone in an ERM matter. Part of the reasoning behind this book is to allay those concerns but where do the "horror stories" originate from? Well I think a lot of the apprehension comes from the Shared Appreciation mortgage "scandal" of the 1990s.

Tens of thousands of borrowers were sold shared appreciation mortgages (SAM) in the late 1990s by both Bank of Scotland and Barclays to help them fund retirement, but many are now trapped in unsuitable homes by debts that rapidly increased to many times more than they borrowed.

How it worked:

The owner of a £200,000 house in 1998 would sign up to a SAM and be given £50,000 cash.

If that house were sold in 2014 for £600,000, the owner would be required to hand over £350,000 to redeem the mortgage.

Sale price: £600,000

House value when SAM taken out: £200,000

Increase in value: £400,000

75% of increase in value: £300,000

Original loan: £50,000

Total repayable: £350,000 (a return for the bank of 600%)

Borrowers thought this was a marvellous innovation as it was marketed as a way of getting instant funds without having to involve solicitors as the banks handled everything themselves "in house".

While for normal mortgages Bank of Scotland had a 60 per cent conversion rate from mortgage offer to the funds being drawn, for SAMs they had a 95 per cent conversion rate.

There were only two interest rates which they considered were sufficient for the launch as they were trying to keep things as simple as possible given "some of the product features were complicated enough to communicate as it was."

In fairness to Bank of Scotland, the lender did initially ask that applicants seek advice from a financial adviser or a solicitor to ensure they really understood what they were signing. Applications that came without the input of a financial adviser were sent back. However, solicitors did not have to be involved. Eventually they abandoned allowing financial advisors to be involved as they were suggesting to clients not to take out the products. If you were working in one of those banks and your livelihood depended on these products being successful then I can understand why they would be reluctant to allow anyone to place resistance in their path. Please keep in mind that these products were available in a different time when the amount of regulation in place for financial products being sold to the public was less stringent than those in place now.

Targeting older, cash-poor customers wasn't the only tactic that questions would be raised about today. Bank of Scotland also forced those taking a SAM to sign contracts in just two weeks rather than the three months borrowers were normally given to decide whether to take a mortgage.

In the in the late 1990s, no one expected house prices to rise by as much as they did. The Nationwide house price index shows prices rose by 270 per cent between 1997 and today. A house could double in value in less than two years.

When the loans became available, applicants tended to be in their 50s and 60s. Two decades later, some of these borrowers – now in their 70s and 80s – owe Bank of Scotland hundreds of thousands of pounds for loans worth just tens of thousands when they were taken out in the late 1990s.

There is a group of pensioners who have formed an action group to take proceedings but no proceedings have been issued as yet at the time of writing. Do you think they would have done so if they had solicitors to pursue with healthy professional indemnity insurance policies to claim on? Based on this, that is why the legal profession, financial advisors and financial institutions are wary of ERM matters.

So, if the clients decide that they wish to proceed with an ERM application there are two distinct types of ERM that they can consider.

Lifetime Mortgages

A Lifetime Mortgage involves taking a type of mortgage which does not require monthly repayments, although with some plans rather than roll up the interest the borrower can opt to make monthly repayments if they wish.

The borrower retains ownership of their home and interest on the loan is rolled up (compounded). The loan and the rolled up interest is repaid by their estate when they either die or move into long term care. If the borrower is part of a couple, the repayment is not made until the last remaining person living in the home either dies or moves into care, meaning that both of them are free to live in their home for the rest of their lives.

If they take they take out a Lifetime Mortgage, they can choose to receive their funds in a lump sum or in smaller, regular amounts. There is also an option available to increase the amount they have borrowed as and when they want to, up to the maximum limit agreed with the plan provider. They can also elect to protect some of the value of their property as an inheritance for their family, meaning that they can benefit from releasing equity while still retaining something to pass on to their children. Some people may be able to release larger lump sums due to impaired health or may prefer to make monthly repayment in part, or in full, with an option to roll up at a later date if the monthly repayments became unaffordable.

Home reversion plan

A Home Reversion Plan also allows a borrower to access all or part of the value of their property while retaining the right to remain in their property, rent free, for the rest of their life. With a Home Reversion product the provider will purchase all or part of the house taking into account the age and health of the owners and will provide them with a tax free cash lump sum (or regular payments) and a lifetime lease, guaranteeing them the right to stay in their property rent-free for the rest of their life. There is no day-to-day interference and no restrictions on treating the house exactly as before; as a private home to live in freely.

The percentage they retain in their property will always remain the same regardless of the change in property values, unless they decide to take further cash releases. At the end of the plan their property is sold and the sale proceeds are shared according to the remaining proportions of ownership. In a way this is very similar in style to shared ownership without the need for ongoing payments.

With both a Lifetime Mortgage and a Home Reversion Plan it is possible to give a homeowner some certainty in their future finances. With a Home Reversion Plan the client knows precisely what he/she has parted with and, equally, what has been ring-fenced for later use, possibly to leave in a Will. With some Lifetime Mortgages it may be possible to also ring-fence an element of equity.

However, you need to be aware that Home Reversion Plan schemes are a big risk for your clients and you will not find them being offered by the main ERM financial providers. If you check with your Professional Indemnity insurance providers then don't be surprised to find that they will be wary to offer cover if you undertake that type of ERM matter.

To protect your professional indemnity insurance, your reputation and that of your firm then you must take an advice you give on an ERM matter seriously. In the next chapter we will look at the process that I would suggest you follow when advising clients. So without further ado, let's take a look.

CHAPTER THREE
ADVISING YOUR ERM CLIENTS

Instructions

Firstly, you need to know why your clients have chosen you/your firm. Over the years I am often horrified when asking a colleague "where did that client come from?" to be told "oh I don't know". Wholly unacceptable in my view. For any work you undertake and in relation to ERM cases you must ask. Most clients pick a firm based on recommendation, whether that is from a third party (their IFA) or from someone they know. Often they will choose someone who is considered an expert in their field.

It is important that you know where the client has come from as if they are an existing client your firm might have vital information you should know about them – for example they suffer from mental health issues and are incapable of managing their finances! Again, firms are generally poor at talking amongst themselves and sharing information, so this gives you an excuse to speak to your colleagues in another department.

Once you have established why your clients have come to you it is good to find out who their IFA is. If you know the IFA then great, they will be a good source of referrals for you professionally. If you don't it is worth checking out who they are. They could be a new source of work but it is important you check that they are qualified to give ERM advice. Now I am not suggesting you ask for their CV but a quick check would do no harm.

One of the fundamental differences with ERM cases is that under the rules of the Equity Release Council referral fees are not permitted. This no doubt will cause ice to run through the veins of panel managers, estates agents and broker networks but it is currently the position regarding ERM cases. You must not pay for this type of work. Several organisations have a large majority of the ERM market as it stands at present but expect new entries into the marketplace as ERM becomes more popular as we all get older.

I have mentioned above the Equity Release Council so I feel I should elaborate as to who they are. Virtually all the ERM lenders have signed up to the Equity Release Council's (ERC) code of conduct. The ERC run training courses across the country and events to publicise ERM and to ensure some uniformity amongst the lenders themselves, very similar to UK Finance (or as most of us knew them the Council of Mortgage lenders) in relation to residential mortgages. Their website has all the information that an IFA will be completing along with samples of all the documents used throughout the matter including the Solicitors certificate which we will look at shortly. The ERC are a vital hub as to how ERM will go forward in this country and should be praised for the good work that they do.

The offer arrives

So, the ERM offer has arrived with you and you need to see your clients. One of the fundamental differences between ERM mortgages and other mortgages is the requirement for a solicitor (or licenced conveyancers or legal executive) to see the borrowers face-to-face. Given changes to our lifestyles I expect that video calls will be permitted before long as the norm but currently this will require lender consent which I am told is often withheld.

As with all mortgages it would be wise to check the terms meet with your initial instructions from your client and check to see if there are any unusual conditions that you need to consider. Once you have done that and perhaps sent a written report to your clients on the terms of the same it is a case of arranging to see them.

Please remember that with ERM then the lender will have appointed their own solicitors to act on their behalf so you will solely be advising the borrower not the lender. The lender's solicitors will deal with all the mundane matters such as registration at the Land Registry giving you more time to focus on the needs of your clients.

Where will you see them?

It is not just the mortgage deed that you will need your clients to sign but perhaps more importantly what is known as the "Solicitors Certificate". In essence this is a checklist for you to follow of matters to discuss with your clients. Before they were known as the ERC then the lenders who dealt with ERM formed under a banner known as the "Safe Homes Income Plan Scheme" or SHIPs for short. The solicitors certificate became known as the "SHIPs certificate".

Follow this document, study this document. Stick to this and you will deal with equity release very safely and are unlikely to go far wrong.

A copy of the same can be seen at the ERC website (see links at the appendix of this book) but in short it breaks down into the following sections which I suggest we look through in some detail now:

Section 1 – Certification

Who is going to see your clients? This might sound like a stupid question as surely if they are your clients then it will be you. However, what if they don't live locally to you or it is simply not practical for them to come to you or for you to go to them?

It is possible to send an Agent to see the clients on your behalf. If you have then you need to check that your Agent has a practising certificate and has professional indemnity insurance. You are also saying that they have complied with the ERC rule 8.4. We will look at rule 8.4 at the end of this chapter at which point you may have some concerns about using an Agent.

What if you are asked to act as an Agent? Well for starters don't expect to be richly rewarded. I was often asked when I was at a previous firm whether I would see someone else's clients for the grand sum of £40.00 plus VAT. This is not a typographical error by the publisher here, yes that is £40.00 plus VAT, Forty pounds plus VAT. Around the cost most firms charge for a telegraphic transfer fee for sending funds. You will see when we look at rule 8.4 later why I am wary of advising people to act as Agent for someone else.

Assuming that your clients instructed you as they would like to see you then you need to decide where to see them. You will see most of your clients at your offices I expect. You won't have far to go to see them and will be doing your bit for the environment by not taking your large luxury motor vehicle out on yet another journey to pollute the air that little bit more (apologies to my readers who have non-fossil fuel burning cars).

By their very nature those taking out ERM are going to be older so mobility may be an issue for them. I have often volunteered to see clients at their home. If they don't drive then this may be the only way to proceed with matters. The advantages are that this will probably relax them as you can put them at ease as you are seeing them somewhere they feel safe and you can learn a lot from people seeing them at home. If they say they are looking for ERM funds to repair their roof and you see a hole in the roof you know their words are genuine.

Confirmation of advice

A. Discussing with their beneficiaries

If a client came to see you for a remortgage of their existing residential property and told you they were looking to raise some funds then provided they did not tell you that they were using the funds for something illegal you would not generally ask too many questions. You would certainly not start questioning whether they should be telling relatives that they are taking out the mortgage. However, the solicitors certificate states that you should advise your clients to consider speaking to the beneficiaries under their Will/Estate that they are taking out an ERM.

The rationale behind this is that unlike other mortgages that will be for a finite number of years with monthly payments, ERMs generally don't have monthly payments or a date when they have to be repaid. Repayment will be when the borrowers pass away generally (see before for more details on repayment). What lenders wish to avoid is for the beneficiaries, when the time comes for the loan to be repaid, making "issues". Given the ramifications of the shared appreciation mortgage situation we looked at in a previous chapter, they are keen to make sure that beneficiaries know that they may not be inheriting the sum they expected.

This is a good time for you to politely ask some probing questions. Can I suggest the following for starters:

- Do they have a Will?
- If they do have a Will, when was it made?
- How many children do they have?
- Have they been married before?

- Who are the main beneficiaries under their Will?

People generally are happy to talk about their family. Nearly all parents beam and are happy to discuss their children and what they do. The lenders know that if an ERM is challenged once the property comes to be sold to realise the loan then it will be the beneficiaries of the borrowers Estate who will be challenging the same. Worse still, if your clients have planned to leave all or part of their Estate to a charity then I have to say I have found charities to be the most litigious of organisations. If they believe that they have a chance of earning more monies for themselves they will take action quickly. The rational behind this is quite simple, when a charity relies on legacies as an important way to raise funds/survive in some cases they want to ensure they receive every penny they can. Who can blame them for this stance?

In addition, when your clients' loan becomes repayable then if beneficiaries wish to challenge the circumstances in which the loan was taken out then they may well suggest that you as the acting solicitor were somehow at fault. By following this checklist, I cannot guarantee that you won't face any issues, but it will certainly stand you in good stead that you did all you could and acted appropriately.

As I have said above, ask if they have told the family. If they have, great. It would do no harm for you to offer for the family to raise any queries they may have with you if your clients want. Best to show your clients have nothing to hide. Often I find that the children of my clients are the ones who suggested ERM in the first place or at least they have been involved in discussions to some extent.

On the courses I have run across the country I am often asked by other solicitors "what if they refuse to tell their family/beneficiaries?". Well you cannot force them to do something they don't want to do. However, I think you should certainly make it clear that they should consider doing so and point out the reasons why. A separate letter following your meeting specifically on this point is also a good idea. If there is a clear record of you making your client aware that they should make their beneficiaries aware then your chance of being protected from any future litigation is surely increased.

Pointing out that borrowing against a property has to be repaid would seem to be obvious. Please keep in mind the society in which we live. A packet of peanuts contains a health warning stating "this may contain nuts". Stating the obvious seems to now be essential as what would have been considered obvious to many does not preclude that some people will simply not understand.

At this stage it is also worth describing the other alternatives as mentioned in an earlier chapter as opposed to ERM. I am sure your clients have considered these already but it is worth making sure that you have a record that you have discussed it with them as well. Those of you seasoned in ERM will know that the standard stock reply from most clients is that it is their home and they don't wish to move. However, asking the question does no harm and shows you have considered all their circumstances.

B. Early death

Death is always a difficult subject to discuss no matter what the circumstances. However, it is essentially to point out to your client that if they take the money then pass away shortly thereafter they won't have had much time to enjoy the funds. They will also place considerable costs on their Estate that would not have existed if they had not taken the loan in the first place.

Simple questions/statements I would make to my clients would be:

- Are they going to get the benefit of the same?
- Is it worth it?

- Are they going to use the funds now?

If you have made them aware of this potential risk then you have covered what you need to on the certificate.

C. State Benefits

Very few solicitors who deal with ERM will have much knowledge of state benefits. This is not because they are elite and above such matters but merely because their day-to-day involvement with clients will not usually involve having an in-depth knowledge of the country's benefits system.

In relation to the Solicitors Certificate then provided you ask your client are they receiving any state benefits and warn them that by taking the ERM they may be potentially reducing the amount of state benefits they claim now or in the future, you will have satisfied your duty.

I would highlight a few points quickly on this issue though:

- ERM won't affect any state pension.

- Establish what benefits they get now.

- If the client (and their partner) have total savings and capital of £10,000 or more then the first £10,000.00 is ignored, this is called the lower capital limit.

- Housing Benefit has an upper capital limit of £16,000 so they will not be entitled to Housing Benefit if they have savings and capital above this limit.

- **Items counted in full** include:
  - cash;
  - money in bank or building society accounts, including current accounts that don't pay interest;
  - money in a Tax Free Childcare account (enter 80% of value)
  - National Savings accounts and certificates;
  - income bonds;
  - stocks and shares;
  - property (other than your own home);
  - Premium Bonds.

  Note that any actual income these assets generate is ignored.

  Note that if they own capital jointly with other people they would normally be assessed as having an equal share.

- **Items that are disregarded capital** include:
  - their home;
  - the value of any property occupied by someone who is a 'close relative' if they have reached pension credit qualifying age or are 'incapacitated';
  - the value of a property for up to 26 weeks if they have acquired it to live there, they are trying to sell it, they are carrying out essential repairs or alterations in order to live

there, or they are taking legal advice so that they can live there;

- the value of a former home for up to 26 weeks if they have left because of a relationship breakdown (or indefinitely if their former partner lives there and is a lone parent);

- sale proceeds of their home for up to six months if they intend to buy another home;

- money from insurance claims for up to six months if used to replace or repair;

- money such as a loan or grant to pay for essential repairs or improvements.

- **Other disregards** include:

  - their personal possessions such as jewellery, furniture or a car;

  - their business assets;

  - any life insurance policy which has not been cashed in;

  - the value of a pre-paid funeral plan;

  - any charge for currency conversion if their capital is not held in sterling;

  - any Social Fund grant payments;

  - arrears of certain state benefits;

  - a lump-sum payment received because they deferred drawing their state pension for 52 weeks or more;

- certain compensation payments.

If they deprive themselves of capital in order to increase the amount of benefit they get they can be treated as if they still had that capital. This is called 'notional capital'. This might occur if they give money away to members of their family or buy expensive items in order to reduce their capital.

They will not be considered to have deprived themselves of capital if they have paid off debts or used money for 'reasonable' spending on goods and services.

If they are refused benefit because of notional capital they should seek advice and consider appealing against the decision.

D. Ongoing obligations

These are no different to the types of obligation that one would expect to see in relation to any residential mortgage of any type. These being an ongoing obligation for insurance to be maintained for the building itself and an ongoing obligation for maintenance.

Most lenders will require their interest to be noted on the buildings insurance schedule and to have a certain amount of cover so it is a good idea to make sure your client lets you have buildings insurance details at the outset. Quite often clients will be taking ERM funds as they wish to carry out improvements to their property, for example a new conservatory or general repairs. Remember that as with all residential mortgages then any alterations to the property that is mortgaged should really be run past the mortgage lender first. After all most of the time they will have a large financial stake in the property.

Provided you have made your clients aware of the same then I would consider that this element of the Solicitors certificate has been covered sufficiently.

E. When does the loan become repayable?

There is no easy way to talk about death. Therefore, it is probably best to not hesitate and simply point out that when your client (or second if a couple) has passed away then the lender will expect the property to be sold so that the loan is repaid. This does not preclude their Estate/Executors providing the funds from another source but usually it will require the property to be sold. This is why it is so important that your clients understand that sale of the property will usually be required for repayment. If they are hoping for their children or a third party to inherit the property than ERM will prevent this in most usual circumstances.

Also, you need to ensure that if your client leaves the property for a considerable period of time then the lender will expect the property to be sold and the loan repaid. No lender wishes to have a property unoccupied for a long period of time. For example, repairs may go unattended to or worse still third parties (squatters) could move in to damage the lenders asset as they see the homes which could hold up a sale.

Entering into long term residential care is also something that generally triggers repayment as if that happens then there is probably little chance of the borrower returning to the property. The lender would expect repayment then once the property was sold. Speaking of selling the property then the borrower can do this but the ERM would have to be repaid. The ERM can in theory be ported to another property.

However like all residential mortgages there will be terms attached to porting the mortgage and the lender will need to consent to the same.

Finally, an ERM will become repayable if there is a breach of any of the mortgage covenants. These are your standard residential covenants. For example, a third party living at the property for a period of time not notified to the lender will be a breach of mortgage conditions as would changing the property from a residential dwelling to a night club without letting the lender know first. Now they may well consent to a third-party occupier (subject them to signing the obligatory occupiers consent form to defer any rights they may have gained in favour of the lender) but the latter point is highly unlikely, in my humble opinion anyway, to be approved by the lender.

F. Security of Tenure

Provided that your clients abide by the mortgage covenants then they will be provided with security of tenure from their lender for their lifetime at the property. The fact that an ERM is in place will not affect your clients' rights to remain at the property itself. Again, provided you have pointed this out you will have discharged your duty under the Solicitors Certificate.

G. Financial advice

The Solicitor's certificate makes it a requirement that you tell your client that they are proceeding with the ERM on the basis of the advice provided from their financial advisor. I always tend to ask clients to confirm that they are happy with the advice supplied by their advisor. It is a good idea to ask now, if you have not already done so, how they came by the financial advisor whom they have been working with. If for any reason they say they are unhappy with the advice supplied then I would suggest that you advise them to speak to another financial advisor for reassurance. If they ask you for a recommendation then I would suggest you provide at least three contact names they could try to avoid any suggestion of bias from your side.

Signing the form to confirm our independence and that we have complied with 8.4

So, I have mentioned earlier that when the form is signed by the legal advisor it is all to comply with 8.4 of the Rules published by the Equity Release Council. It might be useful to know what that actually means. 8.4 states:

> *8.4 The Solicitor (whether this is the Advising Solicitor or the Agent Solicitor) who meets the customer face-to-face is required:*
>
> *(a) to witness the customer's (or Attorney's) signature on any documents which are required to be executed as deeds; and*
>
> *(b) to verify (insofar as they are reasonably able to, acting with all due diligence):*
>
> *i The customer's (or Attorney's) identity and signature;*
>
> *ii That the customer(s) (or Attorney/s) has(have) sufficient mental capacity to enter into the equity release contract;*
>
> *iii That the customer(s) (or Attorney/s) is(are) not under any duress or undue influence to enter into the equity release contract;*
>
> *iv That, in the case of joint customers (or Attorneys), each agrees to enter into the equity release contract; and*

> v That, in the case of the equity release contract being entered into by an Attorney on behalf of a customer, the Power of Attorney or Deputyship Order under which the equity release contract is to be made is valid and correctly executed.

So, in brief you are signing to say that your client has mental capacity and is not under any undue influence. Please take a moment to digest that information. How confident are you that you would be able to tell? I do this a lot and I worry I may miss something. Both of these topics we will look at in more detail in subsequent chapters. The significance of these points is fairly substantial.

Equity release is currently self-regulating. It is not the Financial Conduct Authority (FCA) who has come up with this set of rules nor is it UK Finance (Council of Mortgage Lenders as was) who have dictated the same. The Equity release council has no real power. Its position is secured by all the lenders currently in the marketplace agreeing to abide by its rules. If a new lender were to enter the market and choose not to follow the rules set out then 8.4 may no longer be a consideration.

Now by saying this I am in no way endorsing or suggesting that a lender should not follow the rules set out by the Equity release council. The rules provide a framework for lenders, financial advisors and lawyers to work within which show to the wider world that ERM is "safe" to enter into. As looked at earlier there can be no return to the issues caused by shared appreciation mortgages and the rules go someway to protect the borrowers.

Notwithstanding these points 8.4 is far more onerous in my opinion than when solicitors are involved in more "ordinary" mortgage work. Usually the lawyer would sign the certificate of title and know what they were getting into as it is clear from the UK Finance mortgage lenders handbook what they are signing for. The solicitors certificate obligations are more akin to signing an occupiers consent form hence we will look at the leading case on this in a later chapter. A lot of firms I know will not sign occupiers consent forms or personal guarantees but the similarity to ERM work is staggering. Would they deal with or are they dealing with ERM work without realising what they are doing?

In relation to 8.4 (b) (iii) above, the Solicitor who meets the customer(s) face-to-face would not normally expect any other person to be present. In particular, the customer should receive independent advice in the absence of any intended or potential beneficiary, to avoid any duress being exerted by such a person on the customer(s). There may be circumstances where it is reasonable for a person who is not a beneficiary of the proposed equity release to be present in order to assist a customer. Such circumstances might include, for example, where a customer requires help to hear or understand what is being said, or does not speak English as a first language and requires assistance from an interpreter. In any circumstances where a third party is present, the Solicitor should satisfy him or herself that this is at the request of the customer, that the request is reasonable, and that the third party's presence and purpose in being present is clearly documented.

If an interpreter is present then I would strongly suggest that it is someone you have found not the borrower. If they bring a relative or friend then can you be sure that they are relaying the information correctly. If there is an issue later and the same is challenged then your defence will no doubt be stronger if you had an independent third-party present.

Powers of Attorney

Usually you would not expect a mortgage lender to accept documents (security documents such as a mortgage deed) to be signed under a power of attorney. How could you allow someone to sign up to mortgage conditions and repayments required without that person themselves taking out the mortgage to sign the same? It would be madness would it not? I can imagine though that an Estate Agent or sales agent for a new build property developer has probably suggested it to you at some point though!

However, with ERM matters then certain borrowers will be at a time in their lives when signing documents could prove difficult. Say for instance someone had Parkinson's and a POA was in place to allow bank documents for a joint account to be signed. They may well be of sound mind and not under undue influence but merely cannot physically sign.

On this basis it may be that you find that some borrowers do need to use a POA. Provided you see the same, are happy with the points that you need to comply with then even though a POA is being used then you can accept the same be used. This is of course provided the lender is happy to accept the same.

Attendance notes

Once you have seen your clients then you need to make a record of your attendance. Attendance notes were once considered to be privileged documents. By this I mean that if a client requested a copy of their file they were not entitled to the same. Now with the advent of Subject Access Requests being available for any personal data an organisation may hold against you I suspect that may not be the case.

Nevertheless, your attendance note could be your best form of defence if in the future something goes wrong and you are challenged about how the ERM was handled. On that basis your attendance note needs to be made as quickly as possible following the meeting.

Everything regarding the background of the matter and information you learn during the course of your meeting with your clients should be noted in the same. It is fine (and dare I say encouraged) to follow a template to ensure that you remember to have everything covered. It certainly would do no harm to follow the layout of the Solicitors certificate. This sets out all the points that the Equity Release council suggest should be followed and I think this is a logical way to set out your attendance note.

Keeping a detailed record of your meeting with your clients in turn allows you to write a detailed report letter to them.

Written report

There is no requirement that you confirm what was discussed with your clients in writing. However, to not do so is clearly opening up the opportunity for the same to be challenged at a later date. I would suggest that a written report to your clients is therefore essential.

I would suggest this should cover all the points discussed covering each point in the solicitors' certificate whilst recapping the main terms of the ERM offer itself. Certainly, mentioning the figures and rates of interest are a must.

Personally, I send the borrowers a copy of everything they have signed. I think it helps them to remember what they have signed to and reduces the likelihood of any uncertainty of what they have signed up to as well. I would definitely send by itself a copy of the table from the ERM offer showing how the compound interest will apply to the loan over the years. This is a great visual tool for making it clear to a borrower how much will eventually have to be paid back. It is a proven fact that visual reminders have more effect than the written word (save this book of course!)

Your report letter is your chance to reiterate that they should consider letting their relative or eventual beneficiaries know about the ERM being taken out. It also allows you the opportunity to reinforce that they should feel comfortable in relying upon the advice they have received from their IFA. I am sure that in the vast majority of cases they can and will, but it allows you the chance to remind them that they still have options

I could use this book as a chance to provide a specimen attendance note and report letter which I have considered doing. However, I feel that would be in my style not yours and people are always more comfortable writing in their own style as opposed to someone else's. I do believe this is important in all areas of law. Provided the legal content is correct then I don't see why style should be an issue. Everyone is different and this needs to be remembered as well as embraced.

Completion

Once you have seen your clients then most will want funds drawn down as quickly as possible. This will involve you liaising with the lenders solicitors. It should not prove to be an arduous process.

The vast majority of ERM providers use a handful of panel solicitors and have done for some time. They have procedures in place that you have to follow. A lot of solicitors I speak to seem to find them painful, but I am not sure why. I suspect it is because they don't like being told what to do! It is relatively simple in my mind. Provide what the lenders solicitors want, and your will receive the monies for your client.

One of the advantages from a borrower's solicitors' point of view is that all the usual mundane paperwork that needs to be carried out following completion (registering the charge at the Land Registry for instance) is carried out by the lenders solicitors.

Once you have funds it is a case of accounting to your clients for the funds received and taking your fees. If you have not already done so then this is a good chance to consider offering other services to your client.

So, we have run through one way to approach seeing a client and advising on an ERM all the way from start to finish. We should just finish here shouldn't we?

As you will have noticed lots of issues can arise from an ERM. The next two chapters address two of the major issues that I think arise. Rule 8.4 states that we are checking the mental capacity of the borrowers and that they are not under undue influence. These are not generally areas of law that the majority of the readers of this book will be used to, so I think it is vitally important that we take a look at those areas in more depth.

First up – mental capacity.

CHAPTER FOUR
MENTAL CAPACITY

The **Mental Capacity Act 2005** states that a person lacks <u>capacity</u> if they are unable to make a specific decision, at a specific time, because of an impairment of, or disturbance, in the functioning of mind or brain.

About two million people in England and Wales are thought to lack capacity to make decisions for themselves. The population as of 2016 was estimated to be sixty-five million. That means that three percent of the population of the UK lack the capacity to make decisions themselves. That is a very high number when you think about it.

Do you think you have the ability to spot the same? I always recount this tale when I run courses on ERM. One day many years ago I had arranged to see three sets of clients throughout the day. Not that unusual I know but stay with me.

At 8am I was seeing a client purchasing a new build property from a national developer. Standard for the time but unusual for the time of writing in that it was a fully completed property so was ready for occupation. Once I had run through everything with the client and had them sign the relevant paperwork our conversation turned to when she would like to complete. When I asked whether she had any specific dates in mind she told me 24th April. Now at the time this was not a Friday and usually I find residential clients ask for a Friday to have the weekend to unpack etc.

When I asked why this specific date she replied quite simply, "It's Barbara's birthday". Now I was slightly thrown at this point given that we had just run through that she was going to be living in the property by herself. I replied with "Barbara?" and her response with a quizzical look to me was "Barbara Streisand" as if I should have known. Needless to say, my subsequent response of "of course" I am to this day I am not sure impressed my client.

Thinking that was a slightly odd meeting I went into my midday meeting with my second set of clients for the day. They were a young couple buying a new family home to cope with their expanding family. Their three-month-old son and three-year-old son were in attendance. Now our meeting lasted thirty minutes and during the course of their entire meeting their three-year-old son literally was bouncing off the walls. Dashing this way and that, grabbing my pen trying to crayon the wall and generally causing his parents much embarrassment.

They told me that they had no idea why he was so active. Far be it from me to criticise but during our meeting they gave the young lad two energy drinks designed for those who participate in vigorous sporting activity. At least that is what the labels on the bottles said.

Bemused by this I moved into the afternoon hoping my 6pm meeting would be less eventful. The couple I saw last that day were buying their first home, were engaged to be married the next year and both had what would be considered professional jobs. Thankful for less drama in a meeting all was going well until I asked innocently if they had plans for one of the three bedrooms in the property that had a slightly odd layout.

Mr responded to say that was for a certain female's name. When I asked who that female was he huffed, and Miss went on to regale me with how much she loved that certain female name. It transpired that Miss was a massive fan of a a certain diminutive Australian born pop singer. She had a large collection of paraphernalia linked to said star and wanted somewhere to keep it. Clearly there was tension between the couple over the same.

Now what do the three interlinked stories have to do with ERM? Well on the face of it nothing save that when I told colleagues of these meetings they all asked if these people had mental capacity issues. I am not for any second suggesting that they had but it made me think. Would I at that time be able to spot mental capacity issues in a client?

I consider myself a property lawyer (I would like to say playboy billionaire philanthropist but that is some way off) and capacity is not something I have to address day on day. Private client lawyers have to confront this more often due to the nature of their work. They are therefore very familiar with the Golden Rule.

The Golden Rule

If a person is suffering from certain ailments or have mental health issues then their decision making can be affected adversely. All of the issues we are about to look at surround best practice for the making of Wills and the case law that has swirled around Wills that have been challenged. Now I appreciate this is a book for those involved in ERM but at present there is no reported case law in relation to the same.

However, I am sure you will agree with me that possible challenges are likely to come from the two issues mentioned at the end of the last chapter. Mental capacity we will look at in this chapter and undue influence in the next.

When it comes to capacity issues the "Golden Rule" will apply, but what actually is it? For starters it is not really a rule. You should know by now that us British love giving official sounding phrases more respect than we should. For example "common law husband/wife" has no legal significance.

The Golden Rule in essence requires a solicitor to have respect to the frame of mind and mental capacity of the client instructing them to make a Will. There are many factors which can affect mental capacity which we will look at shortly.

The responsibility of a solicitor in this regard is not a new development. In 1975, the 'Golden Rule' was developed in a case called <u>Kenward v Adams Times 29-Nov-1975, [1975] CLY 3591</u> Templeman, J observed that where a solicitor is making a Will for a client and there is any possibility of doubt about that client's testamentary capacity, then as a matter of prudence they should arrange for a medical practitioner to be present at the time of execution. This has subsequently been dubbed "The Golden Rule" – although most practitioners involved in capacity disputes might tell you that as a rule it appears to be honoured as much in its breach as in its observance.

Yet even as a rule of good practice it has been widely approved by the Courts as having the potential to reduce the risk of a claim of lack of testamentary capacity and should therefore be offered to testators as an additional precaution even if not observed.

The rule is expressed to apply to two categories of testator, namely those who are 'aged' or have suffered a 'serious illness', and therefore the next step is to consider which illnesses are 'serious' for this purpose, and how old 'aged' is.

As a matter of good practice, and a valuable method of at least limiting the number of capacity disputes, it is no more than a matter of commonsense and will no doubt continue to be urged upon those responsible for drafting and overseeing the execution of Wills. If properly employed it certainly provides valuable – and most importantly contemporaneous – impartial and medically qualified evidence of the testator's state of mind at the crucial moment when he actually executes his Will. The same can apply to those entering into an ERM.

For example if you have concerns over the mental capacity of a client before you it is best to seek medical advice Now I appreciate that those of you who are Private Client lawyers in certain parts of the country reading this book will laugh out loud at the thought of me suggesting that they should seek medical opinion on a client's capacity. This is because they would tell me it is nigh on possible to have a GP confirm that their patient has sufficient mental capacity to enter into an ERM. Even if they do reply then their response would make the most ardent lawyer proud with the amount of disclaimers that would be attached to the same.

I think it is worth mentioning that you don't just have to consider obtaining an opinion from a GP. Firstly I don't want anyone to think I am deliberately mocking the medical profession here. They have a difficult job and unlike most people reading this book they actually can be the difference between life and death. The reason they can be reluctant to provide a reference to a patient's capacity is solely down to the legal profession making them fear that they could face legal action if they stick their neck on the line to say something.

An alternative to a GP is to seek help from a specialist mental health assessor. There are quite a few firms out there with knowledgeable staff from a mental health professional's back ground in medicine. They provide a cost-effective method of arranging for a third party expert to check the mental capacity of your client.

However, it has never been an infallible means of forestalling a challenge, let alone defeating one. Much depends upon matters which can vary widely from case to case. For example, the degree of the medical practitioner's knowledge of the testator and the extent of his involvement at the time of execution – in particular whether he carried out any diagnostic tests or examination or simply observed and acted as one of the attesting witnesses. Even a medical practitioner with good knowledge of a patient may be fooled by delusions which he cannot detect because they appear on their face rational in the absence of detailed background information. A true expert who is just used to assess mental capacity might avoid the situation in the next case we will look at – <u>Ritchie v Joslin [2009] EWHC 709 (Ch).</u> Before looking at the facts and issues from the case I should point out that Mr Joslin was the executor of Mrs Ritchie's Will and was her solicitor as well as being one of the executors of her Will.

Mrs Mary Ritchie had died leaving the bulk of her estate of £2.5m (save £5,000 to her local church) to the National Osteoporosis Society ('the NOS') and nothing to her four children. The children argued that Mrs Ritchie lacked the requisite testamentary capacity to make her will, based on the fact she suffered a delusion of the mind which affected her decision to leave her estate as she did. Mrs Ritchie recorded with her solicitor that she held the belief that her children had never helped her, that one of her sons had been violent towards her and that some of her children were stealing from her.

Two issues were relevant to the question of capacity:

1) Whether the statements about her children were true; and

2) If they were not true, whether she believed them or not.

The judge found that the allegations made by Mrs Ritchie, between the death of her husband in 1992 and the execution of her will in 1998, about her children were not true. He also found that the medical evidence suggested that Mrs Ritchie was suffering from paranoia and believed the allegations to be true. There was no rational reason why Mrs Ritchie would have disinherited her children and it followed that the delusions caused Mrs Ritchie to disinherit her children. The will was therefore invalid for lack of capacity. The will was set aside and NOS lost their legacy – the estate passing to the four children under intestacy rules. One can imagine the charity was not happy.

As mentioned in an earlier chapter, charities often rely upon legacies to survive. If they lose out then I expect that cases pursuing potential losses may follow eventually.

Given the relevance of claims challenging the validity of wills on grounds of capacity it is worth setting out the test for testamentary capacity in more detail.

Testamentary capacity

The starting position for any claim is the presumption that an individual has:

1) The competence to make their will; and

2) A continuance of that capacity.

The effect is to require the person disputing validity to prove the individual's lack of capacity – the burden is on them to do so. If, however, there is any 'real doubt' as to capacity, then there can be no presumption of capacity in the first place. This means, the person attempting to prove that the testator was of sound mind when they made their will has to establish this – the burden therefore reverses. The doubt as to capacity must be 'real' and supported by evidence demonstrating a real possibility or probability that the testator lacked capacity – in effect the burden shifts with the evidence. It has been said that the testator should come to a 'rational, fair and just' testament.

In relation to the Ritchie case it is worth mentioning that the Judge paid great attention to the attendance notes that Mr Joslin had made. They were copious and very detailed. He had met regularly with Mrs Ritchie for ten years, so it is fair to say he knew her well. Nevertheless, this did not prevent the Will being overturned.

The test that each party will have to refer to when testing the evidence was set out in the case of *Banks v Goodfellow* – a case decided in 1870, but which is still good law today. It established four key tests for determining testamentary capacity.

Banks v Goodfellow was established as "good law" and to be followed over the Mental Capacity Act 2005 in the recent case of James v James and others [2018] EWHC 43 (Ch*)*.

I think it is important to make this point. The judge in the James case pointed out that the five principles of the Mental Capacity Act 2005 should be look at, but the test to be followed is that as set out in *Banks v Goodfellow*. As the judge pointed out, if the Government did not want the well-established test in a case from 1870 to be followed then surely they would have passed legislation to that effect.

Just briefly the five principles set out in the Mental Capacity Act 2005 to take into account are:

1. A person must be assumed to have capacity unless it is established that they lack capacity.

2. A person is not to be treated as unable to make a decision unless all practical steps to help them do so without success.

3. A person is not treated as unable to make a decision merely because they make an unwise decision.

4. An act done, or decision made under the Act for or on behalf of a person who lacks capacity must be done or made in their best interest.

5. Before the act is done or decision is made regard must be had to whether the purpose for which is it is needed can be as effectively achieved in a way that is less restrictive of the person's right and freedom of action.

Now although *Banks v Goodfellow* is the test we should be following (see below) the five statutory principles above I think can help you when seeing an ERM client. If you take each in turn then apply them to the advice you give:

1. Assume at the outset that your client wants to take an ERM because they have the understanding that they know what they are entering into unless you see signs they are lacking capacity.

2. It is your role as an advisor to make sure they know what they are entering into.

3. If your ERM client says they want the monies to buy an expensive Italian sports car you may consider that an unwise decision (as well as being jealous), but it is their choice.

4. Are you acting in their best interests?

5. Have you advised your client to consider raising funds in a different way?

I am not saying that the above is a perfect system, but those five questions are not bad ones as a starting point in assessing your client's position as regards an ERM.

Now case law in relation to Will disputes makes it clear that the testator must have capacity at the time the will is executed. An exception is the rule in *Parker v Felgate* (1883) 8 P.D. 171.

The Rule in *Parker v Felgate* involved a testatrix who had been in the process of giving instructions to her solicitor to prepare a will over a number of interviews, the last alterations being made on 24 July 1882 and 10 August 1882 before the will was engrossed.

On 26 August the testatrix fell into a coma but was roused sufficiently to execute the will on 29 August. In his summing up to the jury, Sir James Hannen put forward three possible states of mind which would be sufficient to establish capacity:

1. If a person has given instructions to a solicitor to make a will, and the solicitor prepares it in accordance with those instructions, all that is necessary to make it a good will, if executed by the testator, is that he should be able to think thus far, 'I gave my solicitor instructions to prepare a will making a certain disposition of my property. I have no doubt that he has given effect to my intention, and I accept the document which is put before me as carrying it out.'

2. Even if she could not recollect all that had gone between her and the solicitor, she was in a condition, that if each clause of this will had been put to her, and she had been asked, 'Do you wish to leave So-and-So so much?', or 'Do you wish to do this?' (as the case might be) she would have been able to answer intelligently 'Yes' to each question.

3. A person might no longer have capacity to go over the whole transaction and take up the thread of business from the beginning to the end, and think it all over again, but if he is able to say to himself, 'I have settled that business with my

solicitor. I rely upon his having embodied it in proper words, and I accept the paper which is put before me as embodying it'.

Now having looked at all the above let's look at the four well established Tests from *Banks v Goodfellow*.

The four tests of capacity

The four criteria must be separately satisfied. The following are the requirements in more detail:

1. The nature of the act and its effects

This test is very transaction-specific. The testator need not have capacity generally but must have the capacity to execute the particular will under consideration. The approach of the court to the issue of capacity will therefore depend in part upon the complexity of the terms of the particular will. The greater the complexity, the greater the level of capacity required.

The client seeking to make the will must understand:

- that they will die;

- that the will only come into effect on their death and not before; and

- that they can revoke or change the will at any time before death, so long as they remain mentally capable of doing so.

The client must also understand:

- who gets provision from the estate;

- the difference between a conditional and outright gift to a beneficiary under the will;

- that heirs may inherit a great deal more, or less, as the case may be (market values and the testator's expenditure in his final years can affect the size of the estate);

- that the beneficiaries may not survive the testator. The testator may therefore wish to consider substitutional gifts in such an event;

- the executors' role, who they are, and why they should be appointed; and

- whether a previous will has been made and why the new will is different and to be preferred. Sometimes the court will require that a will be explained to a testator to help them understand it, the absence of which means the will is invalid.

2. The extent of the property

This requirement is interpreted in a broad-brush way. There is no need for a testator to be able to compile a mental inventory of all of their assets, but to have a general idea of the assets disposed of by the will.

The client must, broadly, have capacity to understand:

- the extent of their solely-owned property. There is no need for actual understanding of the extent of the assets, only capacity to understand;

- the fact that, regardless of the terms of the will, certain types of jointly-owned property might pass automatically on death to the other joint owner; and

- that there may be pension, insurance or other benefits payable on his death which may not be affected by the terms of the will.

3. The claims to which the client ought to give effect

It is, of course, not necessary that the testator should make provision in their will for persons who have claims upon their generosity, but they must be able to recall them so that they can decide whether or not to benefit them in the will. The testator should therefore be able to comprehend and appreciate these claims and give reasons for preferring certain beneficiaries, and possibly excluding others, for example, by:

- comparing their respective levels of affluence or lack of means;

- assessing any special needs, due to age, infirmity, or disability, which may justify financial support;

- comparing the degree of their care and attentiveness and overall affection and concern for them as an individual; and

- Solicitors should give an explanation of the nature and effect of the will, and to remind their clients of the extent of their assets.

However, in the final analysis, the client himself must be able to appreciate and comprehend the claims to which he ought to give effect without any assistance or prompting.

4. Was the testator's mind affected by any disorder or delusion which was active in bringing about a disposal which the testator would not otherwise have made?

This test is ultimately a question of expert opinion, but the solicitor should exercise his own judgement. For example, as to whether the testator exhibits signs of lack of capacity (by appearing confused for instance) and doubts may be raised if the testator is very ill. If so, the solicitor should follow the golden rule.

So, we have looked extensively at tests for capacity but there are many reasons for mental incapacity. If you are aware of what can cause mental incapacity then you will be better placed to identify the symptoms of the same when they present themselves.

Typical triggers of incapacity

A lack of mental capacity could be due to many factors and I propose to look at some common factors now.

Stroke or brain injury

Given that the majority of stroke victims are over the age of fifty-five years of age and ERM clients have to be over that age, the chances are that you may meet an ERM client that has had a stroke which in turn may have affected their mental capacity. Studies claim to show that those who have suffered a stroke have a greater chance of suffering from some form of mental incapacity including depression and changes of mood.

A mental health problem

If your ERM client has a mental health issue this could affect their mental capacity. As we saw earlier, in the case of Ritchie, the lady in that case was suffering from episodes of paranoia which affected her ability to make rational decisions.

Dementia and Alzheimer's

Dementia and Alzheimer's are the two most common grounds upon which to challenge a will.

This is hardly surprising – dementia and Alzheimer's is fast becoming more prevalent in an ageing population. Claims are often characterised by the beneficiary's relative alleging the testator suffered dementia in the last few years of their life and before the will was made. Statisticians claim that one in ten over the age of sixty-five years of age has Alzheimer's. One in six over the age of eighty years old are claimed to have dementia.

There is no recognised test for dementia, but medical professionals often use a mini-mental state examination (MMSE), with a maximum score of 30, to assess capacity for treatment. These can often be a useful starting point in establishing capacity – a score of anything less than 26/30 indicates dementia. It should be noted however that the severity of dementia is highly relevant – early onset dementia does not usually indicate lack of capacity. A score of 20 to 26 is in the mild range of dementia and it is possible for an individual to have testamentary capacity despite suffering from mild to moderate dementia.

The MMSE involves asking the subject to subtract seven from one hundred and to repeat that several times as in:

100, 93, 86, 79, 72 etc

Or having the subject place two five sided shapes (I know they are called pentagons) to overlap to produce a four-sided shape. The tests are not infallible, but they give some suggestion as to the mental capacity of the subject.

You may well have someone before you who has dementia and or Alzheimer's and never realise they are suffering from the same.

Delusions

Delusions can be a cause of incapacity which can be difficult to rebut. There must be a causal connection between the delusion itself and the disposition effected by the will to establish that individual's incapacity.

A good (although quite extreme) example of a will being set aside because the testator held delusional beliefs is *Kostic v Chaplin* [2007] EWHC 2909 (Ch), Times 11-Jan-2008 in which the testator, a Serbian businessman, left his £8m estate to the Conservative Party Association. He had suffered from a delusional disorder, believing that "dark forces" were conducting a "sinister and highly organised international conspiracy" against him in which various family members were implicated. Part of his delusions involved him believing that only the Conservative Party, through the agency of Margaret Thatcher, could save the country from such dark forces.

Bereavement

Bereavement may produce symptoms equivalent to severe depression. In *Key v Key* the testator made a will exactly one week after his wife's death. It provided for the bulk of his estate to be divided between his two daughters. This was in stark contrast to his previous will, which had left the bulk of his estate to his two sons.

The sons successfully challenged on grounds of lack of capacity and the court accepted evidence that the effect of death can cause the testator to lose the necessary decision-making capacity to make a will. The court observed that the greater understanding of the mind now available from modern psychiatric medicine, in particular in relation to affective disorder, allowed for this development of the test in *Banks v Goodfellow*.

Learning disability

Just because your ERM client may have a learning disability this does not mean that they do not have capacity. I would suggest though that if it is apparent that your client may have a learning disability that you tailor your advice accordingly. Having a second meeting with them to confirm what was said in the first meeting rather than sending an advice letter in writing perhaps. Perhaps having them confirm that they understand things point by point then noting the same with a colleague present may be one way of adding an extra level of protection.

Effects of medical treatment for an illness

Research shows an eighty-five-year-old man costs the National Health Service in England and Wales around seven times on average the cost of a man in his later thirties. Health spending per person increases over the age of fifty years old. Those over the age of eighty five years cost the National Health Service in England and Wales an average of seven thousand pounds per year.

The human body is like a machine. The older it gets the more likely it will need repairs. If you are seeing an ERM client who has had recent surgery or who takes medication for the treatment of a medically diagnosed condition then they may struggle with capacity. If someone is taking strong pain killers for instance then this is likely to have an effect on their decision-making ability. The warning on certain medication that you have all seen that says not to drive or operate heavy machinery whilst taking that course of medication is there for good reason.

Substance abuse

Now you may well baulk at this thought. ERM clients are all respectable home owners but consider these numbers please:

- Between 1992 and 2008, the highest alcohol-related death rates were in men and women aged 55-74.

- In 2008, over one-fifth of older men reported drinking more than four units of alcohol on at least one day of the week, while 10% of older women reported drinking more than the recommended maximum of three units.

- During 2008-2009, 4.8% of over-45s in the UK reported use of an illicit drug in the previous year. The most significant problem for the over-40s was heroin use, either alone or in combination with crack cocaine.

As the population gets older and medical advances are made then the chances are we will see more and more of the older population surviving and dare I say thriving with substance abuse. I accept that it would be rare for you to meet an ERM client carrying a can of extra strength lager whilst carrying a needle, spoon and cigarette lighter. However, substance abuse, alcohol and drugs are an expensive habit so taking funds from their property to fund the same remains a possibility.

What can we learn from these issues for Equity Release?

There is no doubt that challenges to wills on grounds of lack of capacity will increase. The same applies for equity release. The above illustrates the requirements and some common (and some not so common) issues that arise in these cases. Be careful.

There have been no reported challenges as yet, but it is surely only a matter of time. People are far more likely to make a challenge against a Will of a loved one now than ever before.

Charities are extremely fond of threatening and resorting to litigation on probate issues. If an Estate has been reduced by way of an equity release mortgage being taken out then they will more than likely pursue the same.

Making a detailed attendance note following your meeting and being wary of any signs of issues about cognitive ability from the borrowers when you meet them should put you on notice that you might need to assess capacity further.

There are many issues that can cause mental capacity scenarios that you need to be aware of and in reality you probably won't come across more than say one in your career. However as in the case law we have looked at briefly in this chapter, I expect it was likely to be the only matter that the instructing solicitors with each Will had that resulted in each of their matters being scrutinised in the Court then afterwards by the legal world as a whole.

Well, we have looked at the cheery topic of mental capacity that needs to be signed off for 8.4 of the Equity Release Council's solicitors certificate. Now it is probably about time that we looked at the second point they would like to be covered off – Undue Influence.

CHAPTER FIVE
UNDUE INFLUENCE

<u>What is it?</u>

Put simply it is a judicially created defence to transactions that have been imposed upon weak and vulnerable persons that allows the transactions to be set aside.

Now I have a confession to make. I have subjected my children to undue influence. I have failed miserably to get them to support my football team of choice (Newcastle United – Howay the lads!) but I have convinced them that our arch rivals are to be disliked. In fact my influence upon them has actually shown me how easy it can be to ensure that someone acts or says things in one way. To this extent I have let them make their own foolish choices in who to support football wise. We will look at this type of influence, which I will call family influence, again later in this chapter.

More seriously, if someone intends to enter into a transaction, but the intention was produced by means which lead to the conclusion that the intention thus procured ought not fairly to be treated as the expression of the donor's free will, the law will not permit the transaction to stand.

Undue influence and property transactions has a long standing symbiotic relationship in a way. I think this quote sums it up quite well:

> "The striking feature of this appeal is that fundamental misconceptions persist even though the doctrine is over 200 years old and its basis and scope were examined by the House of Lords in depth (in 374 paragraphs) less than 3 years ago in the well-known case of RBS v Etridge. The continuing confusions matter. Aspects of the instant case demonstrate the need for a wider understanding, both

in and outside the legal profession, of the circumstances in which the court will intervene to protect the dependant and the vulnerable in dealings with their property." Mummery LJ Niersmans v Pesticcio [2004] EWCA Cov 372

The test of free will has been expanded upon in *Daniel v Drew* [2005] EWCA Civ 507, [2005] WTLR 807 CA in the speech of Ward LJ (at paragraph 36):

".... in all cases of undue influence, the critical question is whether or not the persuasion or the advice, in other words the influence, has invaded the free volition of the donor to accept or reject the persuasion or advice or withstand the influence. The donor may be led but she must not be driven, and her will must be the offspring of her own volition, not a record of someone else's. There is no undue influence unless the donor if she were free and informed could say 'This is not my wish, but I must do it."

The case of *Daniel v Drew* is an interesting one. In fact, the property in question is not far as the crow flies from my home where I have written this book.

The facts were that a Hampshire farm was left in trust to sisters Ms Drew and Ms Daniel. The sisters gave away their interest to their respective sons. Ms Drew's son had half share, whereas Ms Daniel's sons had one-quarter beneficial interest each. Ms Drew's son acted as de facto trustee on his mother's behalf. The farm was let to Ms Daniel's elder son for what could be described as a nominal sum for years. In fact, he was only paying £1.00 per year. The market rent at the time was considered, which will be no surprise to you as you read this, to be much higher. A figure of £40,000.00 upwards would not have been wrong to consider.

At some stage, Mr Drew wanted rent from his cousin and was prepared to go to arbitration. Mr Daniel claimed repairs in turn. As a compromise, the Daniel brothers would have bought out Mr Drew's interest and Ms Drew would have retired as trustee. However, Mr Drew changed his mind in the last minute. The elder Daniel brother then threatened his aunt with court proceedings. Ms Drew lied to her nephew and said she thought she had already resigned. Mr Daniel wanted a written confirmation, which Ms Drew under reluctance signed there and then before him. There was evidence placed before the Court that Ms Drew did not care much for her nephew. She was intimidated by him and in essence afraid of him.

Ms Drew upon her son's insistence took litigation proceedings against her nephew alleging that her nephew made her resign from her position as trustee of the family trust by undue influence. The first instance judge nullified the resignation. Mr Daniel appealed on the basis that his aunt did not wish to continue in her position as trustee as it was against her interests.

The Court disagreed with Mr Daniel and held that Ms Drew would clearly have wanted to settle the identity of her successor before resigning and obviously wanted her son to replace her. However, Ms Drew was vulnerable and wanted to avoid legal confrontation and in fact any sort of confrontation at all costs. Mr Daniel, a forceful person, took advantage of this and obtained her signature in an unacceptable way.

The key question in undue influence cases is whether the persuasion resulted in the invasion of the claimant's free will. Leading is acceptable but the claimant must not be driven. Here, Ms Drew clearly was not acting at her own free will – as vulnerable as she was, she just wanted to avoid confrontation.

Sadly, there is much case law in this area. Another case to consider is the recent case of *Edkins v Hopkins* [2016] EWHC 2542 (Ch) which demonstrates some of the challenges of succeeding in proving undue influence in relation to a will.

The main beneficiary under a will brought a claim to prove its validity. The main beneficiary had been employed by the testator's company in 1990 and became very close friends with him. The testator had three sons from his first marriage and had hoped they would join him in the business, but he became estranged from them owing to their drug addictions.

He began a relationship with his second wife in 1998. From 2007 they spent a significant time living abroad while the main beneficiary ran the company. The testator developed an alcohol addiction and separated from his wife in January 2013. She visited him regularly, but his health deteriorated, and the main beneficiary began helping him with his financial affairs.

In September 2013 the testator transferred some shares in the company to his wife and indicated to his accountant that he wanted to leave the main beneficiary with a controlling interest in the company itself. He was admitted to hospital a number of times in 2014 with alcoholic liver disease and sometimes displayed confusion. Please remember my words in the last chapter about mental capacity issues caused by substance abuse here.

In June 2014 he decided to change his existing will. The main beneficiary arranged a solicitor's visit. The solicitor noted that the testator looked unwell but believed he had a clear understanding of what he was instructing and signing. The testator died in September 2014, leaving his principal asset, being his company shares, to the main beneficiary, along with 75% of his residuary estate. The remaining 25% went to his wife and sons.

The wife and sons submitted that the 2014 will was invalid because

1. the testator had lacked capacity

2. he had not known or approved of the will's contents

3. the main beneficiary had used undue influence

In terms of undue influence, the testator had been very vulnerable physically and mentally in the time leading up to his signing the will. He had left hospital in May 2014 still dependent on alcohol. Both the main beneficiary and his wife had provided it to him despite the medical conditions he was suffering and against medical advice.

In addition, the main beneficiary had almost a complete degree of control over the testator. He was running the business and taking care of his personal financial affairs. However, that control had to be assessed in the context that it was clear that the testator had placed a great deal of trust in the main beneficiary, as acknowledged to his solicitor and others. This had been in place for a great number of years.

A significant level of that control was given by the testator, not taken by the main beneficiary. The will's instructions were consistent with the testator's continuing desire to leave the bulk of his estate to a friend and colleague who had kept the business going in his absence for some time. He might have been encouraged or even persuaded by the main beneficiary but that had not crossed the line so as to deprive him of his judgement. The Court found that the main beneficiary should benefit as the Will provided.

Two types of undue influence

The case law has determined two distinct types of undue influence.

The difference between the two types of undue influence was captured in *Daniel v Drew*:

> "In the broadest possible way, the difference between the two classes is that in the case of actual undue influence something has to be done to twist the mind of a donor whereas in cases of pre-

sumed undue influence it is more a case of what has not been done namely ensuring that independent advice is available to the donor."

So actual undue influence is akin to my persuading my children that people from a rival football city are less than savoury but presumed undue influence is akin to them not receiving independent advice on the same.

Let us take a look at actual undue influence first.

Actual undue influence

The person alleging that a will was made as a result of actual undue influence must prove it. This can be a difficult task as the main witness is dead and acts amounting to undue influence take place secretively or with very few people present. Many years ago, I laughed on a course I attended where it was suggested that client meetings should have an audio and visual recording made, with consent of course. Having considered this again in my more mature state of mind then notwithstanding the cost involved it might not be a bad idea. I wonder how long it is until professional indemnity insurers insist upon the same?

Undue influence involves overpowering another's judgment as opposed to lesser acts such as persuasion. For instance, my wife persuaded me that we should have a cat rather than using Machiavellian means, at least I assume she persuaded me.

Where actual undue influence is concerned, the claimant will need to show evidence of the actual relationship between the testator and the person accused as the vantage point from which the accused was able to exercise the influence.

For actual undue influence coercion needs to be shown: Wingrove v Wingrove (1885) 11 P.D. 81). This case speaks of someone being coerced into doing something they would not otherwise do.

Sir James Hannen in this case said:

"To be undue influence in the eyes of the law there must be – to sum it up in a word – coercion. It must not be a case in which a person has been induced by means such as I have suggested to you to come to a conclusion that he or she make a will in a particular person's favour, because if the testator has only been persuaded or induced by considerations which you may condemn, really and truly to intend to give his property to another, though you may disapprove of the act, yet it is strictly legitimate in the sense of its being legal. It is only when the will of the person who becomes a testator is coerced in to doing that which he or she does not desire to do that it is undue influence.

The coercion may of course be of different kinds, it may be in the grossest form, such as actual confinement or violence, or a person in the last days or hours of life may have become so weak and feeble, that a very little pressure will be sufficient to bring about the desired result, and it may even be that the mere talking to him at that stage of illness and pressing something upon him may so fatigue the brain, that the sick person may be induced, for quietness' sake, to do anything. This would equally be coercion, though not actual violence.

These illustrations will sufficiently bring home to your minds that even very immoral considerations either on the part of the testator, or of someone else offering them, do not amount to undue influence unless the testator is in such condition, that if he could speak his wishes to the last, he would say 'this is not my wish, but I must do it'.

There remains another general observation that I must make, and it is this, that it is not sufficient to establish that a person has the power unduly to overbear the will of the testator. It is necessary to prove that in the particular case that power was exercised, and that it was by means of the exercise of that power, that the will such as it is, has been produced."

Some poignant quotes come from the case of *Hall v. Hall* LR 1 P&D 481:

"Persuasion is not unlawful, but pressure of whatever character if so exerted as to overpower the volition without convincing the judgment ..., will constitute undue influence, though no force has been either used or threatened"

And

"Overt acts of improper pressure or coercion, such as unlawful threats...

A relationship where one has acquired over another a measure of influence or ascendancy of which the ascendant person then takes unfair advantage... without any specific acts of coercion."

Now before worrying too much, the courts have established that there must be facts demonstrating that actual undue influence has taken place. As well as that there must be reasonable grounds for assuming the same. Keep in mind that there will be costs implications for those who bring unsubstantiated claims.

Allegations of undue influence centre on a relationship which involves trust and confidence (e.g. lawyer and client, doctor and patient, business advisor and client). It has been recognised that such relationships create an opportunity to influence the testator in cases involving Wills and numerous other matters. It is a good time to remember that in all ERM matters, the advisors both legal and financial must remain as impartial and independent as possible.

Now it's time to look at presumed undue influence.

Presumed undue influence

Please note, where wills are concerned there is no claim based on presumed undue influence. However, I don't think this would be the case if a claim was brought due to borrowing for an ERM being induced by undue influence.

Relying on a presumption of undue influence may be seen as something of a secondary line of argument from our friends who are litigators. If someone is struggling to demonstrate actual undue influence one could instead rely on the presumption which shifts the burden of proof to the defendant. This rule relies on demonstrating facts which call for an explanation, which if not rebutted by the defendant will mean the claimant will succeed.

Looked at another way, presumed undue influence is still actual undue influence but where the burden of proof has shifted to the defendant to rebut the presumption.

The presumption arises from showing the following:

(a) certain types of relationship involving a history of undue influence; and

(b) a transaction which requires explanation.

There are some relationships where there is a presumption of _influence_ (be careful to distinguish from _undue influence_). For example, parents over children and future husband over future wife.

The question becomes whether that influence was exercised to such a degree as to be unlawful.

Surprisingly, the presumption does not apply to husband and wife. Those of you that are married may not find that to be too shocking.

In *Yerkey v Jones* (1939) 63 CLR 649, 675 Dixon J explained the reason:

> *"The Court of Chancery was not blind to the opportunities of obtaining and unfairly using influence over a wife which a husband often possesses. But there is nothing unusual or strange in a wife, from motives of affection or for other reasons, conferring substantial financial benefits on her husband. Although there is no presumption, the court will nevertheless note, as a matter of fact, the opportunities for abuse which flow from a wife's confidence in her husband. The court will take this into account with all the other evidence in the case. Where there is evidence that a husband has taken unfair advantage of his influence over his wife, or her confidence in him, 'it is not difficult for the wife to establish her title to relief'"*

This leads us nicely to the recent case that many of you will be familiar with of Royal Bank of *Scotland v Etridge* (No 2), HL [2001], 4 ALLER 449.

Etridge advice

The case was a series of co-joined cases where spouses were seeking to overturn financial charges taken against the matrimonial residential properties. The financial charges in question had been taken out by both named parties on the legal title but the benefit of the charge was for one of the parties as opposed to both.

In *RBS v Etridge* the House of Lords summarised the types of relationships in which a presumption of influence would arise:

> "certain types of relationship in which one party acquires influence over another who is vulnerable and dependent and where, moreover, substantial gifts are not normally to be expected. Examples of relationships within this special class are parent and child, guardian and ward, trustee and beneficiary, solicitor and client, and medical adviser and patient. In these cases, the law presumes, irrebuttably, that one party has influence over the other."

The categories of relationship are not a closed list. Where a trusting relationship has been established between the relevant people a presumption can arise.

Assuming the presumption passes the burden of proof in the direction of the defendant, what must be shown is that the independent judgment of the testator in doing what he/she did was overcome (which is more than showing the testator had understanding).

What about the transaction? There is confusion here and tests are inconsistent. Be wary about looking for a transaction which is disadvantageous to the donor, although in the right case it would undoubtedly help. Applying such a threshold can lead to injustice. What needs to be looked for is a transaction which looks inexplicable, irrational, or calls for an explanation in all the circumstances of the case. In ERM cases it is therefore vital you ask why they want the funds.

The test in law is straightforward. Are there facts in this case that could lead a court to infer that there had been in due influence and nothing else?

The easiest way to rebut the suspicion is to prove that the testator received independent legal advice. One must remember that it is the frailty of the testator which is being protected. So, even where a testator has received independent advice before making a will, the negative influence of the undue influence can still have procured that outcome.

This was emphasised in *Wright v Hodgkinson* [2005] WTLR 435 :

> *"But unless it is shown, whether as a result of independent legal advice or otherwise, that his intention was the result of full, free and informed thought, it is no answer in a case such as the present to demonstrate that he intended to make the gift in question; nor is it a sufficient answer that he might have gone ahead, even if he had received full and proper advice."*

It is not necessary for the solicitor to advise the testator whether or not they should make the will. Nor can the testator be prevented from making a will which appears foolish if he or she wishes to do so.

It is sometimes argued that a transaction would have proceeded in any event despite the undue influence.

Such arguments are wrong in law. This is summed up well in *Hewett v First Plus Financial Group* [2010] EWCA Civ 312 :

> *"It has never been part of the proof of undue influence that, but for the relevant abuse of trust, the impugned transaction would not have been entered into. The right to set aside the transaction arises not because, on a but for causation analysis, it would otherwise have been avoided, but because of the equitable wrong constituted by the abuse of confidence was part of the process by which the victim's consent to it was obtained. In the present case that wrong is constituted by Mr Hewett's breach of his duty of fairness and candour to his wife, when persuading her to agree to the remortgage."*

The separate categories of undue influence have though been criticised in the Etridge case:

> *"Correspondingly the attempt to build up classes or categories may lead to confusion. The confusion is aggravated if the names used to identify the classes do not bear their actual meaning. Thus, on the face of it a division in to cases of "actual" and "presumed" undue influence is illogical. It appears to confuse definition and proof. There is also room for uncertainty whether the presumption is of the existence of an influence or of its quality as being undue..... English law has identified certain relationships where the conclusion can prima facie be drawn so easily as to establish a presumption of undue influence. But this is simply a matter of evidence and proof. In other cases, the grantor of the deed will require to fortify the case by evidence, for example, of the pressure which was unfairly applied by the stronger party to the relationship, or the abuse of a trusting and confidential relationship resulting in for the one party a disadvantage and for the other a collateral benefit beyond what might be expected from the relationship of the parties. At the end of the day, after trial, there will either be proof of undue influence or that proof will fail, and it will be found that there was no undue influence. In the former case, whatever the relationship of the parties and however the influence was exerted, there will be found to have been an actual case of undue influence. In the latter there will be none."* (Lord Clyde)

The case makes it quite clear that a solicitor who gives independent advice will be the agent of the client and not the Bank. More of an onus is put on the Bank to give advice as to the nature of the transaction and then strongly urge that they receive advice from a solicitor. Unless there is a conflict of interest, illustrated by exceptional circumstances then the Bank's or borrower's solicitor may give the advice, although the House of Lords recognised that this would be rare.

The Bank would explain the reason for seeing a solicitor and once the guarantor has decided upon one, they should (with the borrowers' consent) give details of financial history to the solicitor. If the solicitor does not receive such details they should refuse to act.

The solicitor's role is not to veto the transaction but to explain why they are advising and what the nature of the guarantee agreement is. They should also see if the client wishes to try to re-negotiate the transaction and explain the financial position of the borrower. Once more, if the client wishes to go ahead, unless there are exceptional circumstances, they should report accordingly. They should not report to the Bank until the client has agreed.

The House of Lords held that in order for banks to have a valid security interest, they must ensure that their customers have independent legal advice, if they are in a couple where the loan will be used solely for the benefit of one person. Hence why lenders in ERM matters require a separate solicitor to advice the ERM client and another acts for them.

A bank is "put on inquiry" that there may be the risk of undue influence or misrepresentation, if they transact for security over a domestic home, but the loan will only benefit one person and not the other. The solicitor who would give independent advice, however, could also be acting as a solicitor for the bank, or both a husband and wife (or either partner).

The solicitor would certify that he or she was satisfied that both borrowers had given their fully informed and true consent, although if this ultimately turned out to be wrong, the bank's security would not be affected. <u>Instead, the possibility of an action in professional negligence against the solicitor would arise</u>. This would be a personal action, and so it would not help the family stay in their home. The appeals of Etridge, Gill and Coleman were dismissed. The appeals of Harris, Wallace, Moor, Desmond Banks & Co and Bennett were allowed. Lord Bingham gave the first judgment, remarking that the principles set down in the opinion of Lord Nicholls commanded "the unqualified support of all members of the House."

Lord Nicholls held that if the banks ensured that the wife had had independent advice, they could not be responsible for that advice being defective.

The presumption is rebutted if there is 'expression of… free will'. The idea of manifest disadvantage for presumed undue influence was rejected but replaced (like the milder tone in *Allcard v Skinner*) with a transaction that 'calls for explanation', or one which 'is not readily explicable by the relationship between the parties. In the ordinary case it is not 'to be regarded as a transaction which, failing proof to the contrary, is explicable only on the basis that it has been procured by the exercise of undue influence.' That is because it is nothing out of the ordinary. You are put on inquiry whenever a wife offers to stand as surety for her husband's, or a company's debts, where the loan is only going to be for the husband's purposes. Once on inquiry, the bank must ensure that the spouse has independent advice and a certification that they have formed a truly independent judgment.

Etridge was quite a ground-breaking case in that it examined undue influence in some depth. It had such far reaching consequences that banks have tightened up their requirements in relation to lending and are insisting on advice being given independently to most borrowers regarding commercial loans. The Law Society have produced an excellent letter regarding the advice that should be given in the circumstances that I suggest we consider below.

The Law Society model letter

Summary:

All conveyancing solicitors should be certain that before advising on third party charges:

- they have the necessary expertise.
- there is no conflict.
- there is no suspicion of undue influence or impropriety.
- the bank provides full financial information, the advice covers, at the very least, the core minimum requirements.
- the advice is confirmed in writing.

In addition, the solicitor should check if the firm's indemnity insurers have any additional requirements or have issued any guidance.

Finally, it is up to the solicitor to exercise his or her skill and judgement in each individual case to decide whether to act. A solicitor who is acting for the borrower should not agree to advise the third party if there is a real possibility that the advice would be that the third party should not execute the charge/guarantee or consent to mortgage.

The Law Society Model letter can be found online at: http://www.lawsociety.org.uk/support-services/advice/articles/model-letter-post-etridge/

So, what does all of this have to do with Equity release?

If you have husband and wife before you who wish to borrow under an ERM to repay debts incurred by one of them rather than both then I would suggest you have an Ettridge situation. If that is the case then I would strongly suggest that they are seen separately, and separate advice given which is reported back to your lenders solicitors, with your clients consent of course to let the lender know this.

It may not just be undue influence between the borrowers which could be an issue, third parties need to be considered. If the children of the borrowers are pestering them for monies this is something you need to consider. It could be a non-relative. The list is somewhat endless. However, you do not want your assistance to a client undertaking an ERM to be challenged for undue influence, either actual or presumed, at a later date.

Well, we looked at mental capacity and undue influence as required under the solicitors certificate, what I suggest can be called the last check you should make/consider before funds can be released. It is important that you always keep these two issues in mind. I have mentioned about all the challenges that could be made in relation to wills which is akin to ERM but what about if the ERM affects the financial position of the borrowers' beneficiaries. Can they challenge the same and if so how? Let's take a look in the next chapter.

CHAPTER SIX
WHAT IF SOMEONE DOES NOT MAKE PROVISION IN THEIR ESTATE?

Even if the will is valid, certain relatives and dependants can challenge the division of the estate under the will (or the rules of intestacy), by claiming under the Inheritance (Provision for Family and Dependants) Act 1975 (the 1975 Act) that it does not make 'reasonable financial provision' for them.

The categories of those who can make a claim are:

- a spouse or civil partner;

- a former spouse or civil partner who has not remarried or registered a new civil partnership (provided a court order was not made at the time of the separation that specifically prohibits them from bringing such a claim);

- any person cohabitating with the deceased as 'husband and wife' for at least two years immediately prior to the deceased's death;

- a child of the deceased;

- a person treated by the deceased as a 'child of the family';

- any other person who immediately prior to the deceased's death was being maintained by the deceased.

There are statutory guidelines the court must take into account when considering a claim under s.3 of the 1975 Act. These are:

- the financial needs and resources of the beneficiaries and applicant(s);

- any obligations and responsibilities the deceased had towards any applicant or beneficiary;

- the size and nature of the estate;

- any disability (physical or mental) of any applicant or beneficiary and any other matter, including the conduct of the parties.

In the case of an application by a spouse or civil partner, the court will also have regard to the age of the applicant and the duration of the marriage or civil partnership, and the contribution made by the applicant to the welfare of the family of the deceased.

While spouse and civil partners do not have to show that they are in financial need, or were financially dependent on the deceased, to successfully bring a claim, other categories of applicants will need to do so. The maintenance standard is applied, and the standard of provision is 'such provision as would be reasonable in all the circumstances to maintain the applicant'.

The leading case is *Ilott v Mitson and Others* (2015) EWCA Civ 797. The 'maintenance standard' can make it difficult for financially independent adult children to successfully bring a 1975 Act claim against their late parent's estate. Many reports suggest that the Court of Appeal's ruling in the recent case of *Ilott v Mitson and Others* (2015) could now make it easier for 'disinherited' adult children to succeed in bringing a claim.

In this case Mrs Ilott brought what was ultimately a successful claim under the 1975 Act against the estate of her late mother, Melita Jackson. Mrs Jackson deliberately made her will excluding Mrs Ilott and giving her estate of approximately £480,000 to three animal charities.

The Court of Appeal concluded that, as Mrs Ilott had not been financially dependent on her mother, there was no obligation to provide an income to fund Mrs Ilott's needs, but that no provision at all was undoubtedly unreasonable in the circumstances.

A key factor was that Mrs Jackson had no particular association or interest in the three named charities, and had selected them as beneficiaries, so that her estate went to them and not to her daughter, rather than for any positive connection with them.

In determining what amount to award Mrs Ilott, the Court of Appeal held that Mrs Ilott's financial resources were at such a basic level that they offset the fact that she was an adult child living self-sufficiently. The eventual award was of approximately £163,000. This meant that Mrs Illott could purchase her Housing Association property but would not lose her 'no housing' state benefits. The Court was clearly very sympathetic to Mrs Ilott and, in some people's opinion, contrived to ensure that she did not miss out.

This case has been publicised in the popular press as making it easier for financially independent adult children to succeed in bringing a claim. In reality, though, the courts determine each case on its own facts. When analysed carefully, this case is merely the application of the provisions of the 1975 Act to the particular circumstances.

Had the late Mrs Jackson actually had some involvement with the charities, and/or had Mrs Ilott's financial situation been even more favourable, the case may have had a different outcome.

The case does however remind us that although people can still choose to disinherit their children, they will have to have good reasons for doing so, and it would be sensible to carefully document those reasons in some detail.

What has this to do with ERM?

Why mention this in a book about ERM then? The 1975 Act is unlikely to be used as means of challenging an ERM that has been taken out. Other avenues, namely an issue regarding mental health, undue influence, poor financial advice or professional negligence against either the financial advisor or solicitor involved are far more likely.

However, one thing that an ERM obviously does is reduce the amount of money available to someone's Estate when they pass away. Think of the claims mentioned in an earlier chapter regarding shared appreciation mortgages. If the Estate of a "loved one" has become substantially diminished because of an ERM then the beneficiaries are likely to feel aggrieved and more inclined to bring a claim. My point is to keep in mind that an ERM has far reaching consequences once it has been drawn down. I think it is important to keep making this point so that advisors realise the potential consequences from them allowing clients to enter into these transactions.

Now let's look finally at something which on the face of it should be not controversial – joint ownership of property. What has that to do with ERM I hear you shout? Well let me tell you.

CHAPTER SEVEN
JOINT OWNERSHIP

Well, what do we mean by joint ownership?

On the face of it this is the classic joint tenants v tenants in common situation on the legal ownership of a property. The differences can be summed up as follows:

Joint tenants

As joint tenants (sometimes called 'beneficial joint tenants'):

- you have equal rights to the whole property

- the property automatically goes to the other owners if you die

- you cannot pass on your share of the property to anyone you choose as you can in your Will if you held the property Tenants in common

As tenants in common:

- you can own different shares of the property

- the property does not automatically go to the other owners if you die

- you can pass on your share of the property in your will or the laws of intestacy if you do not have one

That all seems quite straight forward doesn't it. The sad thing is that I have been in the law for a long time now. Have I mentioned I used to be thin and have hair? In my experience, no matter how many clients I have seen over the years, and no matter how often this is brought up, this never ceases to be a matter of contention. Until recently, failing to register the title correctly with the type of joint ownership was the most common claim for professional negligence against conveyancing firms.

Now call me cynical but I don't think the average buyer considers the seriousness of this when buying a property. Nor do I think that lawyers in the past did either. When I have a couple of buyers before me buying their first home I always discuss how they would like to hold the property and use this bad rule of thumb. If they say joint tenants then immediately hug, hold hands or make some sort of affectionate gesture I honestly fear for their relationship as sadly I have seen so many of those couples come back in the future to instruct on the sale of the property as their relationship has broken down. On the other hand, those that consider tenants in common, particularly those who ask for a declaration of trust seem to have relationships which last with their other half.

Now the above is just my biased view and what does this have to do with ERM? Well stay with me and I will explain but first let's take a look at some cases law. The following cases are matters where the Courts have been asked to consider whether the property should be classed as joint tenants or tenants in common when the title clearly states it is held as joint tenants.

First up is the case *Jones v Kernott* [2011] UKSC 53. I always feel that when recounting the details of this case that it is helpful to imagine some quiet romantic mood music in your head. Got that record playing quietly now? OK then, we will begin with the facts.

Ms Jones and Mr Kernott met in 1980. In 1981 Ms Jones bought a caravan with the help of a bank loan, and in 1984 Mr Kernott moved into the caravan with her upon the birth of their first child.

In May 1985 Ms Jones sold her caravan, and the parties bought 39 Badger Hall Avenue, Thundersley in Essex, for £30,000. Ms Jones contributed £6,000, and the balance was raised by an interest-only mortgage. The house was conveyed into their joint names. From this point on they shared payment of the household bills and the mortgage. In 1986 the couple's second child was born. The parties took out a loan for £2,000 for an extension which was mostly constructed by Mr Kernott.

In 1993 the couple separated, and Mr Kernott left Badger Hall Avenue. He stopped paying his share of the bills, and contributed little or nothing towards the maintenance of the children. In May 1996 the parties cashed in a life insurance policy and divided the proceeds. With his share of these Mr Kernott bought 114 Stanley Road, Benfleet in Essex, for £57,000.

In May 2006 Mr Kernott sought payment of his half-share of Badger Hall Avenue. Ms Jones responded by claiming under the Trusts of Land and Appointment of Trustees Act 1996 (TOLATA) for a declaration that she owned the entire beneficial interest in the property. Judge Dedman, after considering *Oxley v Hiscock* [2005] Fam 211 and *Stack v Dowden* [2007] 2 AC 432, held that while the interests of the parties at the outset might well have been that the property should be split jointly, those intentions had altered significantly over the years. He considered that the correct test was therefore what was "fair and just" between the parties, taking into account the whole course of dealing between them. He concluded, taking into account Mr Kernott's ceasing to pay any bills, the fact that Ms Jones contributed over 80% of the equity, and the lack of assistance provided by Mr Kernott relating to the maintenance of the children, that the correct split would be 90:10 in favour of Ms Jones.

An appeal was made to the Court of Appeal where it was held that the property should be held equally between the parties as tenants in common.

The resulting appeal to the Supreme Court, saw the highest court in the land overturning the Court of Appeal. It was held that Mr Kernott and Ms Jones would hold the shares in the house on trust in a ratio of 10% to 90%, to reflect their contributions to the home.

Although the Supreme Court unanimously reached the decision, their Lordships concurred on different grounds. Lord Walker, Lady Hale and Lord Collins concluded that there are situations where it would be permissible to impute common intention, while Lord Kerr and Lord Wilson preferred to base their opinions on the fact that the court had the discretion to acknowledge constructive trust in such a manner because it was fair.

The case establishes the following:

i. the starting point where a family home is bought in joint names is that they own the property as joint tenants in law and equity;

ii. that presumption can be displaced by evidence that their common intention was, in fact, different, either when the property was purchased or later;

iii. common intention is to be objectively deduced (inferred) from the conduct and dealings between the parties;

iv. the court is entitled to impute an intention that each is entitled to the share which the court considers fair having regard to the whole course of dealing between them in relation to the property; and

v. each case will turn on its own facts; financial contributions are relevant but there are many other factors

'So what?' I hear you ask. Why should we care about how the equity in a property is shared/split when dealing with an ERM case? Well put simply you may not care but the lender does. More and more ERM lenders are asking for an extra requirement from their borrowers.

This requirement is that the property when in joint names is held as beneficial joint tenants. If the property is held as tenants in common, then they expect the title to be changed to remove the tenancy in common declaration and standard Land Registry form A restriction. If the same is not confirmed, then they are not prepared to offer the loan.

On the face of it this seems quite draconian. Why should the lender have the right to demand how ownership of a property is constructed in practice? After all they have a charge over the legal title to the property and with joint owners they will be jointly and severally liable as one would be advising all mortgage clients where there is more than one person named on the charge.

The difference between an ERM charge and any other residential charge is that most other residential mortgage lenders have a charge that is for a set period of time. The lender is expecting that charge to be repaid either at the end of the term or as usually happens at some point during the term. Again, with most residential legal charges, the capital on the loan is either repaid with interest each month by the borrower or at worth the interest itself is repaid with the capital sum remaining the same.

With an ERM then the lender is expecting the loan with few exceptions in the current market, to be repaid when both of the named borrowers have passed away. The monies due to them on the fixed rate of interest will become repayable when both borrowers are dead.

The lenders concern is that unlike ordinary residential mortgages there is an inherent risk that they may not get their funds. Other residential mortgage products don't require a solicitor generally to sign to say that the borrowers have mental capacity and are not under the pressure of undue influence.

If a property is held as tenants in common lenders take the view that there is potential risk to their security. For example, it could be that the borrowers are on a second or third marriage for example. The property may be held in unequal shares as there are multiple beneficiaries from previous marriages. If this is the case the lender does not wish to take the risk that beneficiaries wish to argue that "their share" should not be affected by the charge in place.

In all likelihood this will never happen as a court would surely see that the charge was against the whole property. However, this could involve lengthy legal battles. The lenders want to realise their monies sooner rather than later. Whilst I have some sympathy as to why they are anti-tenants in common, and now some are asking parties to agree not to change to tenants and common in the future, this is giving the lender a huge amount of power.

Those of you who are private client lawyers or financial advisors will realise that holding a property as joint tenants removes the chance for potential tax savings to clients. Is it right that lenders can, by offering ERM, have this degree of control over the future destiny of their borrowers?

I do feel that this is a serious issue that will come to a head with lenders soon rather than later. At present ERM matters are not commonplace but are growing day by day as the population gets older. As more and more people take the products available I fear that the issue over how a property is held by borrowers will become more contentious.

To protect yourself in such circumstances you need to inform your client that by taking the ERM they are limiting what they can do with the property in the future regarding joint ownership. Some lenders are providing literature to this effect now when they issue their ERM offer.

On that point, it is obvious from the legal title to the property when there are two borrowers. What if it is not obvious that someone else may have an interest in the property?

Is anyone else living there?

Lenders in CRM cases ask the borrowers to confirm that no one else is in occupation of the property. If they are then they will ask that they sign an occupiers consent form. This in reality is no different to how most residential mortgage lenders would treat the situation.

However, I do consider it is worth considering what "someone else living there actually means. The case which I think sums up what it means to have an overriding interest in a property protected by the Land Registration Act 2002 is Chhokar below.

In Chhokar v Chhokar [1984] FLR 313, the husband, who was sole registered proprietor, sold the matrimonial home to which the wife had made financial contributions, whilst she was in hospital giving birth to the child of the marriage! I appreciate this sounds something like a soap opera plot line, so I think consideration of the facts in the case would be in order.

Mr and Mrs Chhokar married on 18 April 1975. In May 1977 Mr Chhokar bought 60 Clarence Street, Southall, for the purchase price of £9,250.00 with a deposit of £700. Mrs Chhokar substantially contributed to the family finance with the sum of approximately £3,000.00.

After purchasing the property, it became apparent to them both that there were matrimonial difficulties and they both travelled to India to visit their parents. Mr Chhokar tried to abandon Mrs Chhokar in

India, but Mrs Chhokar returned in November 1978, a few weeks later.

In December 1978 a friend of Mr Chhokar, Mr Parmar, visited the house pretending to be a potential lodger. Mr Chhokar and Mr Parmar signed a contract of sale for the property for £12,700.00 which due to inflation at the time was actually at an undervalue.

The date of completion was fixed at 12 February 1979. This was no random date. This was the date on which Mrs Chhokar was scheduled to deliver the second child of the marriage in hospital.

However, Mrs Chhokar did not deliver on 12 February 1979. She gave birth on the 16th and so the Mr Chhokar and Mr Parmar agreed to delay the completion of the sale until then. Mr Parmar then put the house on the market for £18,000.

When Mrs Chhokar returned, she discovered the locks had been changed. She broke in but was forced out by Mr Parmar who threatened and assaulted her. Mrs Chhokar managed to gain entry to the house again and stayed in place.

Putting aside the horrendous behaviour of Mr Parmar and the incredibly awful action of Mr Chhokar the question for the court to decide was whether Mrs Chhokar could be said to be in 'actual occupation' even though she was not physically present in the house at the time of the transfer (sale).

Not surprisingly, the court found that, even though her absence the wife remained in actual occupation. Cumming-Bruce LJ:

> *"In my judgment, the guiding principle in the exercise of the court's discretion is not whether the trustee or the wife is being reasonable but, in all the circumstances of the case, whose voice in equity ought to prevail. . . .*

...and I would apply that test to this case. So, we have to decide, having regard to all the circumstances, including the fact that there are young children and that the debtor was made bankrupt on his own petition, whose voice, that of the trustee seeking to realize the debtor's share for the benefit of his creditors or that of the wife seeking to preserve a home for herself and the children, ought in equity to prevail. . . . Nevertheless, there is a discretion. . . .

The voice of the wife sings the following song: 'I became tenant in common in equity with a 50% interest in this property, the matrimonial home, upon its acquisition. I have lived there ever since, subject to very brief periods of absence, and there I have been living with my family. I was deserted by my husband for some years, but I stayed on in the matrimonial home. He has been very unsatisfactory. I had at one stage to obtain an injunction against him to stop him pestering me, but we are now more reconciled. I have agreed to his returning to the home. From time to time he comes there. . . .' and, on the judge's finding, when the case was over he might settle with her again permanently. So, her song is: 'This is the matrimonial home, I wish to continue to enjoy my rights as tenant in common in the undivided share of the house.' She told a lot of lies in the witness-box, which naturally offended the judge because her lies made it more difficult to discover the truth and do justice. It is not unknown for persons with strong grievances to try to embroider their case by telling lies. But when the true facts emerged, there is nothing in her conduct which points to any reason at all for interfering with her continued enjoyment of her equitable rights, including the right to occupy the house, the matrimonial home, and including, if this unsatisfactory husband is willing to continue to live with her there, although he has lost the legal estate, and if she is prepared to put up with him being there, her enjoyment of the matrimonial home together with her husband.

> *Everything that [Mr Parmar] did from first to last in connection with the transaction is stamped with immoral stigma."*

Now I would be surprised if your average ERM clients were likely to be away from the property because they were giving birth to a child, but you do need to ask if someone else is living at the property. Would you wish to have an issue with the lender at a later stage if you knew someone else was resident and this was not disclosed?

On the other hand, in <u>Abbey National Building Society v Cann [1990] 1 ALL ER 1085</u>, the House of Lords held that a person could not be said to be in actual occupation and could not therefore have an overriding interest which bound a mortgagee, when, as an act of grace, the vendor had allowed her to move her belongings into the property 35 minutes before completion.

The facts in Cann are less likely to make the plot line for a new soap opera though. George Cann lived with his mother, Daisy. She had contributed to the purchase price of the home, and so George held the house on trust for himself and her, even though it was solely registered in his name.

They moved to a smaller house that cost £4000 more in a more affluent local area. To buy it they used the proceeds of selling their "home" and got a mortgage from the Abbey National. For younger readers that is now the bank Santander.

Daisy knew the mortgage was necessary. She did not know that George had also taken another mortgage for £25,000.00. Later he could not repay, and the lender wished to repossess the property. Daisy, whose new partner was also living there, argued that she had a right to remain in the home, because her equitable proprietary right arose before Abbey National's, and this coupled with her actual occupation gave her an overriding interest.

Now if this has been their home, as in the previous property they lived in for many years, I expect her argument would be very strong, think Ettridge from an earlier chapter. However, her claim to occupation was based on the fact that she had started to move in carpets thirty-five minutes before the charge was completed. Abbey National argued that when the house was bought with its loan, her right could not arise before.

The House of Lords held that Daisy was not only not in actual occupation, but also that when the house was purchased with the mortgage, Daisy's proprietary interest could not realistically be seen to arise before the building society's. They stated that actual occupation had to have some degree of permanence or continuity. Acts of a preparatory nature, carried out by courtesy of the vendor, were not enough. Think of the potential implications of you having a friend round to help you paint a wall to assist you for instance.

Lord Oliver said the following.

> *"The reality is that, in the vast majority of cases, the acquisition of the legal estate and the charge are not only precisely simultaneous but indissolubly bound together. The acquisition of the legal estate is entirely dependent upon the provision of funds which will have been provided before the conveyance can take effect and which are provided only against an agreement that the estate will be charged to secure them. Indeed, in many, if not most, cases of building society mortgages, there will have been, as there was in this case, a formal offer and acceptance of an advance which will ripen into a specifically enforceable agreement immediately the funds are advanced [sic] which will normally be a day or more before completion."*

However, in Cann it was said that occupation by a caretaker or company representative would satisfy the section. ERM clients are naturally older and therefore as mentioned earlier we are prone to more ailments and may need assistance. If someone was resident at an ERM clients' property to provide medical assistance then I think it would be important to ensure that they should sign an occupiers consent form.

In Hypo-Mortgage Services Ltd v Robinson [1997] The Times, 2nd January the Court of Appeal held that an infant child's occupation of land was a mere shadow of its parents' occupation. It could not give rise to an overriding interest in land even where the child had contributed to the purchase and thus had a beneficial right in the land. It is unlikely that your ERM client will have an infant child, but the next case is more of a possibility.

In Link Lending Ltd v Bustard [2010] EWCA Civ 424 a mentally incapacitated beneficiary who was in permanent care was held to continue being in actual occupation and thus had an overriding interest under Schedule 3, paragraph 2 Land Registration Act 2002. The beneficiary would return under supervision on special occasions. They were held to be in occupation.

The facts in Bustard hark back to undue influence that we looked at earlier. Through fraud, Mrs Noreen Hussein took advantage of Ms Susan Bustard's mental handicap by having her transfer her house in 2004. Bustard was sectioned in 2007 and put in hospital.

Hussein obtained on the 2004 date an interest-only mortgage loan secured against the property approved by HSBC. In 2008 the fraudster replaced her mortgage loan with one from Link Lending and then defaulted, and the lender claimed possession, arguing Bustard had not been there for over a year.

The Judge at first instance found in favour of Mrs Bustard and said that the lender could not have possession. However, given the importance of the decision and possible long-term implications the matter was appealed. Mummery LJ's judgement was fairly scathing in relation to the lender:

> "…..25. The facts are not all one way. Some of the primary facts point against Ms Bustard's actual occupation of the Property at the relevant date: she was not personally present in the Property on 29 February 2008; she had been in a residential care home since January 2007; she was incapable of living safely in the Property; and her visits to the Property were brief and supervised.
>
> 26. Some of the primary facts point to Ms Bustard's continuing actual occupation of the Property: it was her furnished home and the only place to which she genuinely wanted to return; she continued to visit the Property because she still considered it her home; those who had taken responsibility for her finances regularly paid the bills, such as the community charge, from her funds; she was in the process of making an application to the Mental Health Review Tribunal in order to be allowed to return home; and no-one took a final and irrevocable decision that she would not eventually be permitted to return home.
>
> 27. Whether Ms Bustard was in "actual occupation" of the Property at the relevant date was an issue on which the trial judge had to make an evaluation based on his findings of primary fact. As for the law he considered the relevant authorities on the concept of a "person in actual occupation" of land in the earlier Land Registration legislation and now found in the 2002 Act. The construction of the earlier equivalent provisions by the House of Lords is binding on this court. The trend of the cases shows that the courts are reluctant to lay down, or even suggest, a single legal test for determining whether a person is in actual occupation. The decisions on statutory construction identify the factors that have to be weighed by the judge on this issue. The degree of permanence and continuity of presence of the person concerned, the intentions and wishes of that person, the length of absence from the property

and the reason for it and the nature of the property and personal circumstances of the person are among the relevant factors.

28. This court can only interfere with the judge's decision on that issue if it is satisfied that, in the light of the law, it was wrong as a matter of statutory construction, or if it was wrong as a judgment of fact and degree. As for construction, the judge considered the relevant provisions and cited the relevant authorities as to what, in law, is capable of constituting actual occupation of property. As for his application of that law to the facts, the question for this court is whether the judge could properly and reasonably conclude that Ms Bustard was in actual occupation of the Property at the relevant date.

29. In my judgment, this court should not disturb the decision that Ms Bustard was a person in actual occupation of the Property. The judge did not misconstrue the 2002 Act or the authorities. Nor did he misapply the law by making an insupportable evaluation of Ms Bustard's situation regarding the Property. The decisions of the courts on the different facts of other cases have been cited against his conclusion, but they do not demonstrate that he was wrong.

30. The assistance given in the authorities is in clarifying the legal principles, exploring the range of decisions available to the court and identifying the factors to which weight should be given. It is clear from the citations that Ms Bustard's is not a case of a "mere fleeting presence", or a case, like Cann, of acts preparatory to the assumption of actual occupation. It is also distinguishable from Stockholm, which involved the domestic living arrangements of a Saudi princess living with her mother in Saudi Arabia and owning a house in London, where there was furniture and clothing and caretaking arrangements in place, but where she had not lived for more than a year. In this case the new and special feature is in the psychiatric problems of the person claiming actual occupation. The judge was, in my view, justified in ruling, at the conclusion of a careful and detailed judgment, that Ms Bustard was a person in actual occupation of the Property. His conclusion was supported by evidence of a sufficient degree of continuity and permanence of occupation, of involuntary residence elsewhere, which was satisfactorily explained by objective reasons, and of a persistent intention to return home when possible, as manifested by her regular visits to the Property."

The lender here should have been on notice of the actual occupation of Ms Bustard. Items of hers could be found at the property etc. However no true valuation took place. No surveyor inspected the property, it was merely a drive by. I don't know about you, but I always imagine a surveyor driving past the property slowing down to take a few photographs quickly then speeding away with tyres squealing akin to a gangland style murder.

On a more serious note, if lenders can find a way to blame solicitors and financial advisors for any losses they may suffer from a property not being possible to repossess to realise a loan due to an adult occupier or otherwise, they will. It is therefore important to establish who if anyone else is resident at the property.

Now that we have considered all of the above and the previous chapters it might be a good time to summarise what we have covered.

CHAPTER EIGHT
CONCLUSION

My intention in the previous chapters was not to try to persuade you not to deal with ERM cases. If I have then I profusely apologise. What I hope that I have done is make you aware of the sort of thing that you should be considering when advising a client(s) when dealing with an ERM. If you are aware of the potential pitfalls, if I may call them that, then you are perhaps more likely to spot them.

The aim of this book is to introduce you to the basics of the same. There are numerous cases on each section of the process, better people than me have written similar tomes on Mental Capacity and the law as well as Undue Influence, that could be considered in some depth.

The purpose as I have said is to introduce you to the process involved. I would not consider anyone who has read this book to then consider themselves an expert. As with just about all things in life, dealing with matters first hand is the best way to learn how to do something. A textbook can only take you so far.

I would suggest that you keep this book handy for reference before you see an ERM client. The checklist and method of approaching matters is merely a guide. It is not something that is infallible and won't fit every situation but it is a good starting point.

My top tip would be to remember that each client is different. With ERM work you actually have to ask more questions than you normally would with a client. Take the chance to enjoy getting to know them. Speaking to people in the modern world of social media is becoming a dying art so pardon the pun but use ERM as a chance to keep it alive.

Thanks for reading and good luck.

APPENDIX
EQUITY RELEASE COUNCIL RESOURCES

The Equity Release Council has various useful resources on their website at: https://www.equityreleasecouncil.com/home/ including:

- Statement of Principles from the Equity Release Council:

    http://www.equityreleasecouncil.com/standards/statement-of-principles/

- EQUITY RELEASE COUNCIL RULES & GUIDANCE

    http://www.equityreleasecouncil.com/standards/rules-and-guidance/

- Guidance notes for Solicitors on completing the Solicitor's Certificate are contained in the above document at:

    Appendix D: Solicitor's Certificate and accompanying Guidance Notes

MORE BOOKS BY LAW BRIEF PUBLISHING

A selection of our other titles available now:-

'In My Backyard! A Practical Guide to Neighbourhood Plans' by Dr Sue Chadwick
'A Practical Guide to the Law Relating to Food' by Ian Thomas
'A Practical Guide to the Ending of Assured Shorthold Tenancies' by Elizabeth Dwomoh
'Commercial Mediation – A Practical Guide' by Nick Carr
'A Practical Guide to Financial Services Claims' by Chris Hegarty
'The Law of Houses in Multiple Occupation: A Practical Guide to HMO Proceedings' by Julian Hunt
'A Practical Guide to Unlawful Eviction and Harassment' by Stephanie Lovegrove
'A Practical Guide to Solicitor and Client Costs' by Robin Dunne
'Artificial Intelligence – The Practical Legal Issues' by John Buyers
'A Practical Guide to Wrongful Conception, Wrongful Birth and Wrongful Life Claims' by Rebecca Greenstreet
'Occupiers, Highways and Defective Premises Claims: A Practical Guide Post-Jackson – 2nd Edition' by Andrew Mckie
'A Practical Guide to Financial Ombudsman Service Claims' by Adam Temple & Robert Scrivenor
'A Practical Guide to the Law of Enfranchisement and Lease Extension' by Paul Sams
'A Practical Guide to Marketing for Lawyers – 2nd Edition' by Catherine Bailey & Jennet Ingram
'A Practical Guide to Advising Schools on Employment Law' by Jonathan Holden
'Certificates of Lawful Use and Development: A Guide to Making and Determining Applications' by Bob Mc Geady & Meyric Lewis
'A Practical Guide to the Law of Dilapidations' by Mark Shelton

'A Practical Guide to the 2018 Jackson Personal Injury and Costs Reforms' by Andrew Mckie
'A Guide to Consent in Clinical Negligence Post-Montgomery' by Lauren Sutherland QC
'A Practical Guide to Running Housing Disrepair and Cavity Wall Claims: 2nd Edition' by Andrew Mckie & Ian Skeate
'A Practical Guide to the General Data Protection Regulation (GDPR)' by Keith Markham
'A Practical Guide to Digital and Social Media Law for Lawyers' by Sherree Westell
'A Practical Guide to Holiday Sickness Claims – 2nd Edition' by Andrew Mckie & Ian Skeate
'A Practical Guide to Inheritance Act Claims by Adult Children Post-Ilott v Blue Cross' by Sheila Hamilton Macdonald
'A Practical Guide to Elderly Law' by Justin Patten
'Arguments and Tactics for Personal Injury and Clinical Negligence Claims' by Dorian Williams
'A Practical Guide to QOCS and Fundamental Dishonesty' by James Bentley
'A Practical Guide to Drone Law' by Rufus Ballaster, Andrew Firman, Eleanor Clot
'Practical Mediation: A Guide for Mediators, Advocates, Advisers, Lawyers, and Students in Civil, Commercial, Business, Property, Workplace, and Employment Cases' by Jonathan Dingle with John Sephton
'Practical Horse Law: A Guide for Owners and Riders' by Brenda Gilligan
'A Comparative Guide to Standard Form Construction and Engineering Contracts' by Jon Close
'A Practical Guide to Compliance for Personal Injury Firms Working With Claims Management Companies' by Paul Bennett
'A Practical Guide to the Landlord and Tenant Act 1954: Commercial Tenancies' by Richard Hayes & David Sawtell
'A Practical Guide to Personal Injury Claims Involving Animals' by Jonathan Hand
'A Practical Guide to Psychiatric Claims in Personal Injury' by Liam Ryan
'Introduction to the Law of Community Care in England and Wales' by Alan Robinson
'A Practical Guide to Dog Law for Owners and Others' by Andrea Pitt

'Ellis and Kevan on Credit Hire – 5th Edition' by Aidan Ellis & Tim Kevan
'RTA Allegations of Fraud in a Post-Jackson Era: The Handbook – 2nd Edition' by Andrew Mckie
'RTA Personal Injury Claims: A Practical Guide Post-Jackson' by Andrew Mckie
'On Experts: CPR35 for Lawyers and Experts' by David Boyle
'An Introduction to Personal Injury Law' by David Boyle
'A Practical Guide to Claims Arising From Accidents Abroad and Travel Claims' by Andrew Mckie & Ian Skeate
'A Practical Guide to Cosmetic Surgery Claims' by Dr Victoria Handley
'A Practical Guide to Chronic Pain Claims' by Pankaj Madan
'A Practical Guide to Claims Arising from Fatal Accidents' by James Patience
'A Practical Approach to Clinical Negligence Post-Jackson' by Geoffrey Simpson-Scott
'A Practical Guide to Personal Injury Trusts' by Alan Robinson
'Employers' Liability Claims: A Practical Guide Post-Jackson' by Andrew Mckie
'A Practical Guide to Subtle Brain Injury Claims' by Pankaj Madan
'The Law of Driverless Cars: An Introduction' by Alex Glassbrook
'A Practical Guide to Costs in Personal Injury Cases' by Matthew Hoe
'A Practical Guide to Alternative Dispute Resolution in Personal Injury Claims – Getting the Most Out of ADR Post-Jackson' by Peter Causton, Nichola Evans, James Arrowsmith
'A Practical Guide to Personal Injuries in Sport' by Adam Walker & Patricia Leonard
'The No Nonsense Solicitors' Practice: A Guide To Running Your Firm' by Bettina Brueggemann
'Baby Steps: A Guide to Maternity Leave and Maternity Pay' by Leah Waller
'The Queen's Counsel Lawyer's Omnibus: 20 Years of Cartoons from The Times 1993-2013' by Alex Steuart Williams

These books and more are available to order online direct from the publisher at www.lawbriefpublishing.com, where you can also read free sample chapters. For any queries, contact us on 0844 587 2383 or mail@lawbriefpublishing.com.

Our books are also usually in stock at www.amazon.co.uk with free next day delivery for Prime members, and at good legal bookshops such as Hammicks and Wildy & Sons.

We are regularly launching new books in our series of practical day-to-day practitioners' guides. Visit our website and join our free newsletter to be kept informed and to receive special offers, free chapters, etc.

You can also follow us on Twitter at www.twitter.com/lawbriefpub.

Printed in Great Britain
by Amazon